THE TRIBE
By Jean-Michel Mension
CONVERSATIONS WITH GÉRARD BERRÉBY AND FRANCESCO MILO
Translated by Donald Nicholson-Smith
Contributions to the History of the Situationist International and Its Time, Vol. I

Publication date: November 2001

ISBN: 0-87286-392-1   136pp

Trade paperback original $14.95

Biography/Cultural Studies/Politics

For further information please contact:
Stacey Lewis, publicist
stacey@citylights.com
415 362 1901
James Brook, editor

CITY LIGHTS BOOKS
261 Columbus Avenue
San Francisco, CA 94133
ph 415 362 1901
fax 415 362 4921
www.citylights.com

D0976367

the
tribe

JEAN-MICHEL MENSION

CONVERSATIONS WITH
GÉRARD BERRÉBY AND FRANCESCO MILO

TRANSLATED FROM THE FRENCH BY DONALD NICHOLSON-SMITH

Contributions to the History of the
Situationist International
and Its Time, Vol. I

CITY LIGHTS BOOKS
SAN FRANCISCO

Cover & book design: Stefan Gutermuth/doubleu-gee
Cover photo of Jean-Michel Mension by Garans

Editor: James Brook

This work, published as part of the program of aid for publication, received support from the French Ministry of Foreign Affairs and the Cultural Service of the French Embassy in the United States.

Cet ouvrage publié dans le cadre du programme d'aide à la publication bénéficie du soutien du Ministère des Affaires Etrangères et du Service Culturel de l'Ambassade de France représenté aux États-Unis.

Mension, Jean-Michel.
    [Tribu. English]
    The Tribe by Jean-Michel Mension; translated from the French by
    Donald Nicholson-Smith.
    . p. cm.
    Interviews with Gérard Berréby and Francesco Milo.
    ISBN 0-87286-392-1
       1.Mension, Jean-Michel—Friends and associates—Interviews.2.Paris
    (France)—intellectual life—20th century—Interviews. 3.Radicalism—France—
    Paris. I.Berréby, Gérard. II. Milo, Francesco.III. Title.

    DC715 .M39413 2001
    944'.36083'092—dc21

CITY LIGHTS BOOKS are edited by Lawrence Ferlinghetti and Nancy J. Peters and published at the City Lights Bookstore, 261 Columbus Avenue, San Francisco, CA 94133. Visit us on the Web at www.citylights.com.

the tribe

INTERNATIONALE LETTRISTE

n° 2

manifeste

la provocation lettriste sert toujours à passer le temps.la pensée révolutionnaire n'est pas ailleurs.nous poursuivons notre petit tapage dans l'au-delà restreint de la littérature,où le faute du mieux c'est naturellement pour nous manifester que nous écrivons des manifestes.le désinvolture est une bien belle chose,mais nos désirs étaient périssables et décevants.la jeunesse est systématique, comme on dit.les semaines se propagent en ligne droite.nos rencontres sont au hasard et nos contacts précaires s'égarent derrière la défense fragile des mots.la terre tourne comme si de rien n'était.pour tout dire, la condition humaine ne nous plaît pas.nous avons congédié ceux qui croyait à l'utilité de laisser des traces.tout ce qui maintient quelque chose contribue au travail de la police. car nous savons que toutes les idées ou les conduites qui existent déjà sont insuffisantes.la société actuelle se divise donc seulement en lettristes et en indicateurs,dont André Breton est le plus notoire.il n'y a pas de nihilistes,il n'y a que des impuissants.presque tout nous est interdit.le détournement de mineures et l'usage des stupéfiants sont poursuivis comme, plus généralement,tous nos gestes qui peuvent déposer le vide,plusieurs de nos camarades sont en prison pour vol.nous nous élevons contre les peines infligées à des personnes qui ont pris conscience qu'il ne fallait absolument pas travailler.nous refusons la discussion.les rapports humains doivent avoir la passion pour fondement,sinon la terreur.

sarah abouaf,serge berna, p.j.barlé, jean-l.brau, leibd mibard j'aheu, guy-ernest debord, linda, françoise lejare, jean-michel mension, éliane papai, gil j wolman

notice pour la fédération française des ciné-clubs

éclaircissement sur le film "hurlements en faveur de sade". le spectacle est permanent.l'importance de l'esthétique fait encore,après boire, un assez beau sujet de plaisanteries.nous sommes sortis du sinéma.le scandale n'est que trop légitime.jamais je ne donnerai d'explications.maintenant tu es toute seule avec nos secrets, A L'ORIGINE D'UNE BEAUTE NOUVELLE tu me tiens tard dans le grand désert liquide et borné de l'allée des cygnes (tous les arts sont des jeux médiocres et qui ne changent rien) son visage était découvert pour la première fois de cette enfance qu'elle appelait sa vie.les conditions spécifiques du cinéma permettraient d'interrompre l'anecdote par des masses de silence vide. Tous les parfums de l'arabie,l'aube de villennes, A L'ORIGINE D'UNE BEAUTE NOUVELLE.mais il n'en sera plus question.tout cela n'était pas vraiment intéressant, il s'agit de se perdre.

guy ernest debord

liberté PROVISOIRE

bien sur la nuit tu rêves et tu poursuis toujours dormir mais la vie menace à chaque angle et il y a des flics et des indics dans les bistros les filles de ton âge sont marquées par la jeunesse.

gil j wolman

extraite de la presse à propos de l'affaire chaplin. les feux de la rampe ont fait fondre le fard de soit disant mime génial et l'on ne voit plus qu'un vieillard sinistre et intéressé.(finis les pieds plats-

---

29/10/52.tract lancé par l'internationale lettriste à la réception de chaplin à Paris).

les lettristes signataires du tract contre chaplin sont seuls responsables du contenu contenir et confus (jean isidore isou. combat 1/11/52.)

nous croyons que l'exercice le plus urgent de la liberté est la destruction des idoles,surtout quand elles se recommandent de la liberté...les indignations décrite à isou indifférent.il n'y a pas de degré parmi les réactionnaires.nous les abandonnons à toute suite facile énergie et choqués.(position de l'internationale lettriste.combat 2/11/52)

nous nous posicionnons si peu pour les littérateurs et leurs tactiques que l'inimitié est presque sublétique c'est vraiment comme si jean isidore isou ne nous avait rien dit....(guy ernest debord-mort-d'un commis-voyageur-internationale lettriste N°1)

"charlot" emporte la médaille d'or du cent cinquantenaire de la préfecture de police que lui a décerné hier après-midi mr.jean beylet,ainsi qu'un bâton blanc-breloque qu'il a suspendu à sa boutonnière.(charlie chaplin quitte paris-france-soir 10.11.52)

grève générale

il n'y a aucun rapport entre moi et les autres.le monde convenue le 24 septembre 1953.j'ai dix huit ans, le bel âge des maisons de correction et le sadisme a avili.je respirai dieu. la beauté de l'homme est dans sa destruction.je suis un rêve qui n'aurait pas réussi tout acte est lâcheté parce que justification.je n'ai jamais rien fait.le néant perpétuellement cherché, ce n'est que notre vie. dégustée à savant de valeur qu'un jardinier.il n'y a qu'un mouvement possible. que je suis la proie et décerne les butons.tous les moyens sont bons pour s'oublier-rustiko,picous de mort,drogue,alcoolisme,folie,mais il faudrait aussi abolir les porteurs d'uniforme,les filles de quinze ans encore vierges, les êtres réputés sains et leurs prisons.si nous sommes quelques uns prêts à tout risquer,c'est parce que nous savons maintenant que l'on a jamais rien à risquer et perdre.aimer ou ne pas aimer tel ou telle, c'est exactement la même chose.

jean michel mension

fragments. de recherches pour un comportement prochain.

"la nouvelle génération ne laissera plus rien au hasard."

gil j wolman

de toutes façons on n'en sortira pas vivante.

jean michel mension

l'internationale lettriste veut la mort,légèrement différée,des arts.

serge berna

délibérément au-delà du jeu limité des formes,la beauté nouvelle sera DE SITUATION

guy ernest debord.

INTERNATIONALE LETTRISTE

INTERNATIONALE LETTRISTE No. 2

general strike

there is no relationship between me and other
people. the world begins on 24 september 1934. i
am eighteen years old, the fine age of reformatories
and sadism has at last replaced god. the beauty of
man lies in his destruction. i am a dream that would
love a dreamer. any act is cowardly because it justi-
fies. i have never done anything. nothingness per-
petually sought is, simply, our life. descartes has as
much value as a gardener. only one movement is
possible: that I be the plague and hand out the
buboes. all means are good for forgetting oneself:
suicide, death sentence, drugs, alcoholism, madness. but it is also needful to do away with wearers
of uniforms, girls over fifteen but still virgins, osten-
sibly healthy people with their prisons. if there are
a few of us ready to chance everything, it is because
we now know that we never have anything to
chance or lose. to love or not to love this man or that
woman is exactly the same thing.

jean-michel mension

Impassive man of marble,
he set his foot
on the staircase of that same metal.
Greetings, Guilbert!

You signed this text in Internationale Lettriste *No. 2,
which appeared in February 1953. You were eighteen....*

Yes, but in fact I had arrived in the "neighborhood" younger—I must have just turned sixteen. I
arrived because I disliked whatever was not the
neighborhood more and more, especially high
school, and I was in search of a place where I could
be free. This was a world that I liked because I disliked the world of my parents. My parents were
old Communist militants—old in terms of their
veteran status; they had joined very young. My
father was a full-time Party worker, my mother
was a full-time technical employee of the Party—
a typical sexual division of labor, of course.

It was at the 1933 Fête de l'Humanité [the Communist Party's annual fair—*Trans.*] that Robert Mension and Rose Fuchsmann decided to have a child. At a counterdemonstration on 9 February 1934, pregnant with me, Rose was shot at. They missed us. My first photo shows me, naked, at a Party gathering in Montreuil in June 1935.

What section of the Party were they in?

It wasn't exactly the Party. It was a sports organization, a federation very close to the Communists. My father was the Party's man in the organization.

Where was this?

In Paris. I was born in Paris in 1934, my father was born in Paris, my mother was born in Paris, and ... well, actually, my grandmothers were not born in Paris: one, a Russian Jew, was born in the depths of the Ukraine, and the other was born in Picardy or something of the sort—I'm not sure now.

What was your childhood like with your family before you got to the neighborhood?

It was very bad—but that wasn't my parents' fault, more the fault of the times. I barely remember the prewar years—I was almost exactly five when war was declared. I do have a first memory: we were in a house in the Yonne; I had an operation for appendicitis and my brother broke his arm.... They put a plate in him, and that's how he was identified later, when they found his body at Buchenwald after the war. And I very well remember my father's face when he opened the Communist newspaper *L'Humanité* the day the Hitler-Stalin Pact was announced: he was livid. It was one of my first big shocks. When he came home from the army, my father went underground immediately, which was contrary to Party directives at the time. So I was living with my mother, and one day a woman arrived in tears, saying, "They have arrested Auguste Delaune." You see stadiums named after Auguste Delaune all over France, especially in Communist municipalities. He was the national head of the

FSGT, the Labor Sports and Gymnastics Federation; my father was in charge of the Paris region, and Delaune was a very big friend of his. That was when my mother gave me my first and last lesson in survival, teaching me the fundamental rule, "Never admit anything." She explained that I must say that I had not seen my father since he left for the army. That rule served me extremely well at the time, it served my father well, and me, too, in other circumstances later. On top of everything else, my mother was Jewish, even though at the time she was—well, so un-Jewish. She had joined the Communist youth organization at seventeen. In those days nobody imagined that the Jewish issue would ever become as intense, as dramatic, as it did, so we barely mentioned it. Still, she told me, "If you are asked the question, you say you are not a Jew." I took it all in, and the cops paid us a visit not long afterward; I couldn't have been much more than six, I think it was in October of 1940. They came to arrest my father, who was already gone. They pushed me about a little, twisted my arm—not so much to hurt me really as to throw a scare into my mother, make her crack. But with my mother there was no chance of that. Mission impossible: she was stoic, heroic. There you are, those are my earliest memories, memories of a time that was difficult, because I was being tossed about in the wake of my father's life in the Resistance, living here, there, and everywhere. I also spent time in a sanatorium of some sort.

You mean you went wherever your father went?

No, not at all. My father always refused to leave Paris, even though in principle those who became too well known in any particular region were not supposed to stay there indefinitely. He was the only leader—he was appointed director of the Communist Youth in '43 and held that post from February '43 until the Liberation—he was absolutely the only Communist Youth leader who was never arrested during the Occupation. And the only one to survive. All the others before him died—guillotined, deported, shot.

So you were with your mother all the time?

Not all the time. I was in a nursing home, but I had regular contact with her. We lived together in our prewar place; then when the Nazis intervened in the USSR she also went underground. After that I saw her sometimes, lived with her sometimes. We used to go and see my father in the summer of '41. We would go from Belleville up to Boulevard Serrurier. I had an uncle who lived there, a tailor, Jewish, naturally, and my mother showed me how to make sure the cops didn't follow us.

What did you do?

We would take different routes. I would lag behind, she would go on ahead, things like that. We would go to see him every Sunday when I was there, and we never went the same way twice.... I have no idea whether we were ever followed or not.... The Germans came sixteen times looking for my father. We lived in Rue de Belleville, in lower Belleville, and the seventeenth time they came it wasn't for my father. It was then that the arrests of Jews began, or at least identity checks. That seventeenth time they were looking for my mother. The concierge was very good: my mother was out, so she stuck a note next to the lock saying, "Rose, get out of here quick!" It was pretty brave of that concierge, because the cops might easily have come back before my mother got home. They were good people, and I fancy good concierges like that were pretty much in the minority in those days. Anyway, we were lucky. So much for my childhood: it wasn't that unhappy, but it was a bit rough.

And when the war ended?

I was in the Yonne. Friends, Party comrades, came one day to fetch me. They took me back up to Paris in a van and dropped me off in the suburbs. My aunt came to get me by bicycle—she was in the Resistance, too—and brought me back to Rue Mouffetard, where my parents were living. It was nighttime, and there was still gunfire on the rooftops. I can't say I cared whether there was shooting or not: all I cared about was that I wasn't going to end up an orphan—an issue that had indeed bothered me for much of the Occupation. I was reunited with my parents; we began an almost normal life, looking for an apartment, finding one—in Belleville again, in fact. And then everything started to....

Were you going to school?

Yes, regularly. During the war I only went from time to time, and there were interruptions when I was in the sanatorium or the nursing home. There were courses, there were classes, but we didn't have to go; we learned nothing whatsoever. I was a little bit academically inclined when I was small, but not afterward.

Until you were how old?

Until I cut out. Earlier, even. Until I stopped taking an interest in things of that kind, because I thought

If only the Jews were blue, yellow, or striped, we would not have had to make them wear stars so we could identify them.
RADIO PARIS (JUNE 1942)

that I was being not so much formed as deformed by the system. Until my first year at high school....

You had the feeling that things were going on elsewhere?

Yes, there was a gap—there could only be a gap—between what went on at home and what was going on outside, because my folks were Communist militants, genuine ones, honest, real revolutionaries. My father was a paid official but earned practically nothing; my mother was sick. My little brother arrived in '46, and my mother never properly recovered from the days of the Resistance: she was not working, she was on permanent disability. My father had nothing except his pay from the Party, and we were no longer eating meat. We were living on a very, very tight budget. My father wouldn't believe the people who told him, "Look here, Robert, they're telling you fairy tales—there are plenty of full-timers who don't live like you, you should demand such and such...." No, he had nothing, he took the metro every day still wearing his ancient wartime lumber jacket, even though other officials were already siphoning off a little extra. He never would.

What was your relationship with your parents like? Were they much taken up with their political activities?

Not my mother, though she regretted it. Life circumstances obliged her to give up part of her militant activity, and she always disliked that. My father, on the other hand—we worked it out once—was away from home more than six months out of the year. What's more, he was not a very talkative man; he was hypersensitive, but had great difficulty expressing it. So he and I didn't have much of a relationship to speak of, and that left its mark on me. I was a son of militants, and it wasn't ideal. At home all the talk was political. I never saw non-Communists at home, except for the downstairs neighbor, the concierge who looked in now and then, and the godmother of my little brother, who for her part was not a Communist but who had something of an interesting story because she was Polish. She had fled Poland in 1930 and married to get her papers. That was often done at the time, and, of course, the guy she got married to was a friend from the Party; he was a worker, too, a member of Prévert's "October" group. He died in the Spanish Civil War. So, seeing as her fellow had died in that war, she was allowed to come to our house. Aside from that, though, there was never anything but Communists.

What about your tailor uncle? Was he a Communist, too?

No, my tailor uncle—as a matter of fact, I had two tailor uncles. The one I mentioned earlier was very old, much older than the rest of the family. Among other things, he had been involved with Trotsky's groups in 1905. He was very young during the 1905 revolution and the time of the pogroms. He was more of an anarchist, really. It was he, I think, who founded the French union of tailors working at home; these tailors used to supply Galeries Lafayette, and he organized their first strike in '29 or thereabouts. The other tailor uncle was not a Communist, either, but he had still had trouble in his younger days with the Romanian police. He was a Romanian Jew and as such had fled the country, but then he got stuck in Budapest during Béla Kun's Commune. None of his people were Communists.

They came to the house, then?

Oh, yes, they were family, there was no problem. There was only one member of my family that I never saw at home, and that was my paternal grandmother.

How come?

Because my father was very obstinate, and he had had a falling-out with her one day when he was young. Result, I went all through my childhood without even knowing that I had this grandmother. My father admitted it to me after the death of my mother's mother, which shook him up, because he adored her. She was indeed an extraordinary woman, who brought up seven children completely by herself. So my father got a shock when she died, and that was when he told me that he had a mother, and still living. I was no longer very young myself by then, and my son, my first son, must have been going on ten. So he got to know his great-grandmother and I got to know my grandmother at the same time. That was my father's way—a bit brutal, really. But otherwise there were no real problems in the family. After the war we would get together around the two major Jewish holidays, because that was the tradition. My grandmother no longer went near the synagogue, didn't practice at all. All the same, in her close family—including her brothers and her children—seventeen people had died as deportees, so she went back to the synagogue in their memory. There was nothing religious about it, though, it was just tradition: all the family would come together at her house on those two Jewish holidays.

What was your state of mind when you began frequenting the neighborhood?

My state of mind was also a result, naturally, of my reading. I used to haunt the local public library. I read everything and anything—perhaps even a bit too much of anything. I remember reading the first three volumes of Sartre's *Situations*, things like that. I read Prévert—but the Prévert was a family thing: I had two or three aunts and two uncles who had been members of the October group. One of the aunts had gone on a trip around the USSR with the group in 1930 or just after. I don't know whether it was already called October then; perhaps it was still "Prémices." So Prévert was a kind of family tradition, his name came up at every meeting, invariably apropos of the good old days, when they were young and all that sort of thing. All long before I read Prévert myself. I remember that I read Queneau, Gide; I remember that I read Anouilh, things that I couldn't have found at home, Jorge Amado.... I was lucky enough to have Jean-Louis Bory as my French literature teacher.

Did Bory get you to read particular books?

No, not directly. But he did decide that out of our five hours of French a week he would spend one hour on modern literature, which was not in the program. That's how he got to tell us about Anouilh and Gide, and certainly in that sense you could say that he influenced me, though no more than the other pupils. Beyond that, I was reading things on the side that had nothing to do with what I was learning at school. And I have to say that at the time I was put off when it came to *Le Cid*—I think it must have been in the year before high school—when it was rammed down our throats, and we still hadn't

finished the play by the end of the year: we used to
spend a whole hour on two lines of it, and the
teacher we had was a guy who had cute little cards
that he must have made when he first entered the
profession back in 1920 or thereabouts. I was disgusted, and I am disgusted to this day, at least with
Corneille and Racine; Molière, too, but I got over
that very quickly. Racine and Corneille I can't say I
regret too much; it doesn't matter really.

*Can you say what reading at that time left the biggest
impression on you?*

Yes, I can. It was in the summer of '50. We were
spending our holidays in Briançon, in the Alps. Our
holidays were always pretty much of a muchness;
people from the Party would let or lend us a place.
So that year we were in a little villa near Briançon,
and there was a fine collection of books. I came
upon a certain Arthur Rimbaud, and I confess that
to this day I have not yet finished with him, not
quite. There was Verlaine, too. I read the whole of
Verlaine; it was very beautiful, but not the same
thing at all as Rimbaud. I also read Lautréamont—a
bit later on, but I was still very young.

Was that after arriving in the neighborhood or before?

Before, I think—or just at the beginning. In point of
fact, I arrived first on the other continent, so to
speak: at the Café Dupont-Latin. This was at the
beginning of the new school year, 1950. Before that
I had come into the Latin Quarter a couple of times,
but that was it.... I was still a bit afraid of it.

So with Rimbaud and Lautréamont under your arm, fif-
teen or sixteen years old, you landed in the neighborhood?

That's it. I arrive and start drinking a little.

The first people you met?

The first encounters? Well, they were at the
Dupont-Latin.... It was an immense café taking up
a whole block, with Rue des Écoles on one side and
Rue de Cluny on the other. It was vast. At the time
you could still order yogurt as a drink; people were
still drinking strawberry milkshakes, ghastly things
like that.

Luckily, there were lots of parties in the after-
noons. Young people using their parents' places,
supposed to be at school like me, like all of us. And
there we would drink, quite a lot, in fact. That was
when I really began drinking. My friend Raymond
and I used to pass the hat in these little parties,
then go and buy junk for people to drink, bottles of
entre-deux-mers or sweet wine for the young kids,
who weren't really drinkers at all; and we'd get a
bottle of gin with the surplus funds and keep it to
ourselves, just the two of us. A small first step
down the alcoholic path—that's how it started.
The method didn't last long, but my taste for
alcohol certainly did.

How did people get to know one another?

The real neighborhood was here, at the Café de
Mabillon, on Boulevard Saint-Germain. Not the
Dupont-Latin. The Dupont-Latin was the port, or
the beach, before the great departure; and you had
to cross the Boul' Mich'—leave the Latin Quarter,
was the way we put it—and make the voyage from
the Dupont-Latin to the Mabillon: that was the

Work now?—Never, never, I am
on strike.
I shall never work.
Sapristi, I shall be a rentier.
I have a horror of all trades.
I have a horror of my country.
I do not understand laws.
We will murder logical revolts.
Such toil! Everything must be
destroyed, everything in my
head erased.
I thirst to extinguish gangrene.
ARTHUR RIMBAUD

initiation. Most people got lost, got drowned, on the way over. There were some even who went back home right away, but the vast majority of the people from the Dupont drowned crossing that ocean. Much later, you reached an enormous café full of people just like you, where everything happened very quickly.

The Mabillon, where we are sitting right now?

Exactly. Everyone talked to everyone else. There were quite a few café philosophers, as we called them, people like that, holding forth. At the time I was a bit impressed by them, I must admit. Not least because they were already twenty. They were chatterboxes with their little followings; they had flipped through a few books without usually understanding much. The big fad then was existentialism. People, tourists, used to come to the neighborhood to see the existentialists, and there were a few bozos who would spout off, playing the part, to get a free meal or a free drink. It was a specialty, and some were better at it than others. Fabio was one. He must have passed his baccalaureate in philosophy—he was a truly amazing gabber, also a bass player, the only character I ever met who hitchhiked with a double bass. Another one, similar, was Jean the Poet. Needless to say, he also wrote poems. He became a bartender at the Montana, in Rue Saint-Benoît—a very fancy bar.

You had no money when you arrived in the neighborhood?

No, very little. Officially, I had none at all. My parents weren't giving me any, but, well, you always found people.... Actually, there was a period when we had a lot of money, but it didn't last long. From wastepaper collection. There was a paper shortage, wastepaper was very valuable, and the students would go from door to door leaving a notice announcing that they would call back on such and such a day for any wastepaper. We used to get there ahead of them and pass ourselves off as students.

And you would resell the paper?

Yes, and it fetched a very good price. We were all rich! We went on being rich for a time, then I had to abandon this great racket because some bastards claimed to have seen me dead drunk on Boulevard Saint-Michel.

Pure slander?

I wouldn't say that, exactly. But they went and told my parents, who then tried to get me back on the straight and narrow by packing me off to high school in Beauvais for three months. I made a deal with my mother, saying, "OK, I'll go, but come July you'll get me papers, an identity card, a passport, because I want to go abroad, I want to travel." We both kept our end of the bargain, then I left.

You needed the papers to be independent?

No, no, so that I could go to foreign countries. It wasn't about emancipation: it was always my mother who paid the fine when I got arrested for public drunkenness, which was fairly often.

So you went traveling?

I visited Italy in October 1951. Florence. A wonderful city.

CIVIL CODE, ARTICLE 115: Should a person have ceased to visit his place of domicile or residence and should no news at all of said person have been received for four years, interested parties may appeal to the Court of First Instance to declare this absence formal.

Were you on your own?

Not exactly. I had a dog, as skinny as hell. People would take pity on the dog, then on me by extension, which was very practical. I was gone for three weeks or a month, then I came back to the neighborhood, but I still wanted to wander. So that December I set off for Stockholm with a friend—whom I still see, incidentally, one of the rare people from back then I still see; we're just a handful now. Anyway, we stopped in Brussels, found the beer to our liking, and stayed there for six months.

Drinking beer?

We drank a vast amount of beer, and for my part I wound up in the reformatory after we were arrested.

Arrested for what?

There was a police roundup in the part of town that was the Saint-Germain-des-Prés of Brussels—there was a jazz band there and everything. The cops nabbed us because we were foreigners and we had no papers except our passports—no residence or work papers at all. They caught three of us, but the other two were over eighteen and so they were simply escorted to the border the next day. But I wasn't eighteen yet, and I was sent to a reform school.

How long were you there for?

Forty days—long enough to get the general idea. But this was a Belgian reformatory—half Walloons and half Flemish—and there was nothing but fist-fights from morning to night. I hadn't the remotest interest in all that, I was utterly different from the other fellows in there—all of them petty thieves, rebels, with no families or parents divorced.

What year was that?

March and April 1952.

Your mother came to get you, didn't she?

CHEZ GEORGES, RUE DES CANETTES
PHOTO: GARANS

My mother came to get me, and then I was back in the neighborhood, wearing something of a halo on account of the sojourn in reform school. Normal life resumed—meaning the life of the neighborhood, hitting people up, conning them a bit, stealing a little.... Not really stealing, though, because at the time tons of people used to come into the neighborhood. It was easy pickings—after all, there weren't so many of us all told, a hundred, a couple of hundred, perhaps. People have a false picture of Saint-Germain.... And for us it wasn't Saint-Germain, anyway. I don't suppose I myself have been into the Café de Flore more than twice in my life, and the same goes for the Deux-Magots. For us the neighborhood ended, roughly speaking, just before you get to the statue of Diderot. Across from there was a bar called the Saint-Claude. Just before Rue de Rennes. We used to take Rue des Ciseaux. At the corner of Rue des Ciseaux and Rue du Four was Le Bouquet, and a bit farther on down Rue du Four was Moineau's. On the far side of the street, at the corner of Rue Bonaparte, if I'm not mistaken, was a place that sold frankfurters and fries: La Chope Gauloise. On Rue des Canettes, where we weren't going much as yet, Chez Georges was already there, a well-known bistro. Georges himself hadn't arrived yet, though. We would make our way back via Rue du Four; La Pergola was opposite, and, just a few steps farther down on the same sidewalk, the Old

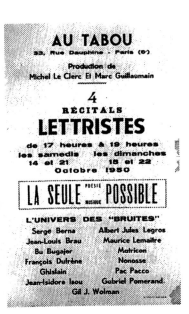

AT LE TABOU

Navy. Then there was another place, slightly farther afield, which seemed in fact very far away to some people; it was across from the Vieux-Colombier theater, but I can't recall its name. Sometimes we ventured as far away as a café called Le Nuage and a couple of other places in a little street on the far side of Rue de Rennes, but that was rare. Occasionally in the evening we would run into people who would invite us out elsewhere, but by and large we congregated around this place, the Mabillon. Here there were only people like us. At the bar, at the end of the room, there might have been a few neighborhood residents, but, of course, we were always at the tables.

You were always sitting at the tables?

In those days, yes. It was only later that we started propping up bars. Here at the Mabillon we were always sitting. There was a place that was important for us late at night—so far away, almost like being deported. That was the Bar Bac. When we weren't totally legless we would make our way to the Bar Bac, and there we would meet people who were not from our own neighborhood, people like Blondin. Late at night, past four in the morning, you found the real hard cases.

What about Le Tabou?

Le Tabou's clientele was more like that of the Flore or the Deux-Magots. The generation before mine. Mind you, when I say generation, it might be a matter of only six months or a year's difference. I did go to Le Tabou a few times, though, yes. Twice, for certain, for Letterist concerts—but by that time everything was practically over. On the other hand, in the very early days, when I was still going to the

Dupont-Latin, we used to go to jazz clubs, like Club Saint-Germain, in Rue Saint-Benoît, but that was not the same, it had nothing to do with the neighborhood in the sense in which I have been describing it. The jazz clubs were not part of that.

So the neighborhood's geographical boundaries were marked by bars?

For me, yes. Not for everyone, but for me definitely. Still, there were certain other places, like Allée du Séminaire at the top of Rue Bonaparte, where we might gather around a bench if we wanted to be a little out of the main fray for some reason, if we wanted a little more privacy. That was where Éliane would meet us, just outside the neighborhood, when she didn't want to be picked up by the cops because she was on the run. Another such place was Square du Vert-Galant. We used to collapse there or panhandle. Debord adored that spot. It was a sort of frontier: we never went to the Right Bank.

You had been hanging out in those bars for a while when you met the people with whom you took part in the Letterist movement. How did that come about?

It was after Brussels, after the reform school. I went on vacation—well, "vacation" is hardly the word: we were on vacation all year long! Anyway, we got back from the Côte d'Azur in September '52.

On vacation with your parents, you mean?

No, no, not anymore. That vacation was with a guy called Joël—who ended badly, I'm afraid.

PIERRE-JOËL BERLÉ

There was in those days, on the left bank of the river (it is impossible to go down the same river twice or to touch any perishable substance twice in the same state), a neighborhood where the negative held its court. GUY DEBORD, *In Girum imus nocte et consumimur igni*

That was Joël who?

Joël Berlé. His actual first name was Pierre. He ended up as a mercenary in Katanga. It was a spiral: he started by stealing more than others, then went on from there, and the rest followed. He was put in the clink, or at least was in grave danger of being put in the clink, for a long time.... I first ran into him when I was shuttling between Paris and Brussels, so he must have reached the neighborhood rather late, in '52. He came from La Ciotat or Marseilles. His official father—later, I burgled his villa with Joël— was at the time head of the shipyards at La Ciotat; his mother was a nice lady. Joël always told me that this was not his real father, that his real father was a guy who wrote detective stories for the famous "Le Masque" series. His mother had supposedly had this gentleman as a lover and separated from her official husband, etc. But I met him at that particular moment, and a couple of days afterward we went to Brussels together. We lived there for a while, then left for the Côte d'Azur during the summer season. We hung about in Cannes for a bit together, misbehaved together. Joël was something of a thief—a lot of a thief, even.... In Cannes we played the gigolo a little, swiped a few things from cars. Small potatoes. Joël wasn't such a serious thief yet, I guess.... Then we went back up to Paris, separately, as a matter of fact, and hooked up again here. Joël didn't know the neighborhood well at all; it was me who brought him in, took him to Moineau's. But then he became one of the gang, one of the tribe. He signed texts of the Letterist International, but he didn't give a shit about that. He took to stealing rather seriously. He had a special technique: he did the rounds of the hotels, only going into rooms if the key was on the door, which was quite often (it was the same with cars—there were still lots of people who didn't bother to lock their cars up). So he could be sure that there were people in the rooms he went into, and he might wake them up. He had to work very discreetly, the result being that he often stole the strangest things, because, of course, he couldn't put the light on. He took whatever he found, an alarm clock, whatever it might be. Once, in the car of a guy with whom we had hitched a ride, he managed to pinch what looked like a fine shirt out of a suitcase. After we were dropped off, I tried the thing on: it was a pajama top! He also found something that turned out to be very useful to us: a bunch of overcoats, some kind of gabardine, which went down almost to your feet. This wasn't the style at all in Saint-Germain, which at the time called for black or for Scotch jackets made from tartan blankets swiped from parked cars. But those coats were marvelous for our raids on the cellar of the bar on the corner. The owner, old Quillet, was something of a character: he felt that his taxes were excessive, so rather than pay the state he closed up shop. His customers went in by the back door, through the courtyard— chiefly old geezers from the École des Beaux-Arts, people like that.

PIERRE-JOËL BERLÉ
ON A MERRY-GO-ROUND
PHOTO: GARANS

You mean it was an illegal bar?

You might say that. Now Quillet had a cellar chock-full of white wine from the Loire, pretty dry—we called it the "exorbitant white"—and we stole cases and cases of the stuff, because he never locked it up. We walked into that cellar whenever we felt like it, and with those vast gabardine coats we could each stick about eight bottles in the pockets. When we couldn't drink the whole haul, we would stash the surplus bottles on a building site down Rue de Buci, for the next day. The earliest to wake up got to drink them.

JEUNESSE ABUSIVE

JEAN MENSION et Auguste Hommel, 20 ans, affrontent le président Royer, à la 12e Chambre correctionnelle.

Leur tenue (nous parlons de leur accoutrement) est curieuse : pantalon en velours côtelé vert-pomme, godasses invraisemblables d'épaisseur. Couronnant le tout, une tignasse hirsute et peut-être habitée. Il paraît que c'est l'uniforme d'une certaine jeune Saint-Germain-des-Prés et que c'est indispensable pour « épater » le bourgeois. Chaque époque a connu des jeunes gens révolutionnaires par leurs mœurs et leurs idées : Incroyables, sous le Directoire ; romantiques sous Louis-Philippe ; cubistes, fauves, avant 1914 ; surréalistes en 1920 ; zazous en 1943 ; existentialistes par la grâce de M. J.-P. Sartre. Mais ces jeunes gens, s'ils faisaient beaucoup de bruit et peu de chefs-d'œuvre, ne volaient pas. Mension et Hommel ont perfectionné le système : non contents d'épater le bourgeois, ils le pillent. Un inspecteur les vit « s'intéresser » aux autos garées boulevard Saint-Germain et dans les rues avoisinantes ; ils avaient alors les mains vides ; il les revit avec des sacs à main, des appareils photographiques... Leurs mains n'étaient plus libres ; eux ne le furent pas longtemps.

J. MENSION et A. HOMMEL

non plus, l'inspecteur ayant emmené le tout, voleurs et objets volés, au commissariat.

On dit — un peu par plaisanterie — que le président Royer ne badine pas avec sa clientèle. Soyons justes : il sait, quand les circonstances le requièrent, doser le châtiment. A ces deux-là, qui ne furent jamais condamnés ; qui pourront travailler lorsqu'ils auront compris l'inanité et l'insanité de leur conduite qui « n'épate » personne, mais qui afflige tout le monde, le président Royer n'inflige que 6 mois de prison, avec sursis et 12.000 francs d'amende.

Dans les couloirs, les deux « héros » retrouvent leur thiase : une dizaine de jeunes hommes, volontairement crasseux, grattant frénétiquement leur tignasse, pour « épater » le photographe et la rédactrice de cette petite cause.

NI PAR LA PLUME, NI PAR L'ÉPÉE : PAR LES BALANCES

TRISSOTIN et Vadius réglaient leurs comptes eux-mêmes et réclamaient, tout au plus, l'arbitrage de Boileau. Plus tard — et plus cruellement — Voltaire et Jean-Fréron disputaient à coups d'épigrammes. C'étaient là de grands siècles où, bien qu'on fût procéssif (Les Plaideurs de Racine le prouvent) on n'appelait pas la Justice à l'aide pour un écrit mal jugé. De nos jours, les écrivains — et même les écrivailleurs — ont, l'épiderme plus sensible. C'est ainsi que Michel Mourry, ce jeune homme qui ne craignit pas de diffamer Dieu, à Notre-Dame, en plein prêche, fut ulcéré par quelques écrits de Georges Arnaud, l'auteur du Salaire de la Peur. Il chargea M. Klotz de poursuivre Arnaud en diffamation. M. Paul Garson, avocat d'Arnaud, s'apprêtait au combat qui devait se dérouler à la 17e Chambre correctionnelle ; il avait aiguisé des armes dont la moindre n'est pas l'ironie spirituelle.

Hélas ! (pour nous) Michel Mourre comprit à temps que la Justice pourrait fort bien ne pas lui être plus tendre dans le rôle de plaignant que dans le rôle d'accusé ; son avocat fit retirer l'affaire du rôle, purement et simplement.

Ce qui prouve qu'on peut être jeune, contempteur de dieux et pourtant avoir des moments de sagesse.

VIOLETTE NOZIÈRES POURRA NOURRIR LES SIENS

LE mois dernier, Me de Vésine-Larue, avocat de Violette Nozières, avait formulé une demande de réhabilitation de sa cliente, cela afin de lui permettre de pouvoir prendre un commerce et nourrir ainsi sa vieille mère et ses deux enfants.

La Chambre des mises en accusation avait repoussé cette demande.

Me de Vésine-Larue, s'appuyant sur la loi du 30 août 1947 qui prévoit des dispenses à l'interdiction de prendre un commerce pour toute personne condamnée à des peines graves, demanda à la Chambre des mises la réhabilitation commerciale.

Statuant en chambre du conseil, sous la présidence de M. de Moissac, et conformément aux conclusions de l'avocat général Raphaël, la Cour d'assises de la Seine, que la Chambre des mises avait saisie de cette demande de réhabilitation commerciale, vient de l'accorder à Violette Nozières.

Cette grande coupable, à présent complètement réhabilitée, pourra donc prendre prochainement un commerce (probablement un hôtel-restaurant dans l'Orne), ce qui lui permettra de sauver de la misère — et peut-être de la mort — quatre personnes.

Qui? Détective No. 363 (15 June 1953)

WAYWARD YOUTH

Jean-Michel Mension and Auguste Hommel, 20 years old, are up before Judge Royer of the Twelfth Magistrate's Court.

Their aspect (we refer to their attire) is very curious, including apple-green corduroy pants and ridiculously thick-soled shoes. To complete the picture, wild mops of thick—and possibly inhabited—hair. This is seemingly the uniform of a particular type of fauna found in Saint-Germain-des-Prés, and it is said to be indispensable for shocking the bourgeoisie. Every period, of course, has had young people revolutionary in their morals and ideas: Incroyables during the Directory, Romantics under Louis-Philippe, Cubists and Fauvists before 1914, Surrealists in 1920, *zazous* in 1943, existentialists courtesy of Monsieur J.-P. Sartre. But at least all those young people, even if they produced lots of noise and very little by way of masterpieces, were not thieves. Mension and Hommel have put the finishing touch to the model: not satisfied with shocking the bourgeois, they rob them, to boot. A police inspector spotted them showing great interest in cars parked on Boulevard Saint-Germain and nearby side streets; their hands, at the time, were empty; later he saw them again laden with handbags, cameras, etc. Their hands, in short, were no longer free. Nor were they free a while later, after the inspector carted the whole lot—thieves and plunder—off to the local police station.

Somewhat jocularly no doubt, it is said of Judge Royer that he pulls no punches in dealing with his "clients." Let us be fair: he knows very well how to weigh the circumstances and when appropriate to show restraint in the penalty he imposes. In the case of these two, who had no police records, and who will be able to work as soon as they come to understand the inanity and insanity of their behavior (which "shocks" no one, by the way), Judge Royer confined himself to six-month suspended sentences and fines of 12,000 francs for each offender.

By and by, in the corridor outside, our two "heroes" rejoin their thiasus—ten or so young men, willfully filthy and frenetically scratching their topknots in hopes of shocking the photographer and reporter of their dreary cause.

Qui? Détective No. 363 (15 June 1953)

HANDS OFF THE LETTERISTS!
Subsequent to who knows what acts of
provocation, Pierre-Joël Berlé has just
been arrested.
He is charged with illegally entering
the Catacombs with intent to
steal lead.
We refuse to take this accusation
seriously.
The real motives involved are
obviously different.
Being determined to defend freedom
of expression in France, we demand
that P.-J. Berlé be released forthwith
and all charges against him dropped.
We nevertheless support any and all
acts of our comrade.
There is no such thing as an
innocent Letterist.
For the Letterist International:
BULL DOG BRAU
HADJ MOHAMED DAHOU
GUY-ERNEST DEBORD
GAËTAN M. LANGLAIS
RENÉ LEIBÉ
JEAN-MICHEL MENSION
GIL J WOLMAN

That was when you and Joël were partners?

Not in his career as a hotel thief. He was on his own
there. I had no talent in that department....

What about stealing from cars?

That I did with Joël, yes. But also with others, after
we came out of the bistro. Once I was caught. I was
given a suspended sentence because of my clean
record at the time. This was something we did pretty often; nor were we the only ones—we thought of
it as quite normal. True, Gil Wolman, Jean-Louis
Brau, and Guy Debord were strictly not involved in
this kind of thing; they were honest (not that we
others considered ourselves dishonest, exactly), but
they certainly never moralized about it.

What was Joël like?

Joël didn't yet have a very clearly defined character.
He was a guy with a great sense of humor, always
thinking up the most amazing things, making
everyone laugh.... Things like hitchhiking out of
town with nothing in his satchel but a telephone
directory. Or cooking up all kinds of schemes. It was
Joël who perfected the system for getting into the
Catacombs. There was an element of barter here,
too: the deal was, he agreed to pilfer the lead from
the lamps down there, and in exchange he was
given the details of an entrance to the Catacombs on
Rue Notre-Dame-des-Champs. At that time lead
was very valuable, and there was indeed a lot still
unfilched down in the Catacombs. He got nabbed
one day emerging from a manhole leading to the
sewers—he had a pretty good knowledge of the
underground geography of the city; there is a
Letterist pamphlet issued in his support on one

occasion. With the lead coiled around him, he must have looked like those old-time bicycle racers wearing their spare inner tubes like bandoliers. He and I would still see each other in the bars, but we were no longer teamed up. After Joël and I split up, he pulled off some bigger jobs, which led to his joining the Foreign Legion to avoid serving a two-year prison sentence. As was fairly common, he was sent to Algeria. Later still, he signed on as a mercenary in Katanga. For a very long time we thought he was dead, and it did indeed turn out that he had been badly wounded in Algeria. Once he paid a return visit to the neighborhood. It was before '68; he stayed a couple of days, then moved on. Joël was an adventurer, but of a different stripe from the adventurers of the neighborhood—even if there were some real crooks, some really colorful types among us. Joël was a thief in a big way, though I gather he pulled back from the brink eventually, that after Katanga and all that he straightened up. I don't know how he did it, exactly—he was headed for a real life of crime.... So, I came back to the neighborhood with Joël, and that was when we all made the move to Moineau's. The second crossing. From here to Moineau's must have been roughly three hundred meters, but this move was even more complicated than the earlier one, and we lost even more people on the way across. Moineau's was a kind of desert island in the middle of....

From the Dupont-Latin to the Mabillon....

Yes, the first journey.

And the second: from the Mabillon to Moineau's.

Which was a very rough winnowing process: people were afraid to go over there.

They were rootless children come from every corner of Europe. Many had no home, no parents, no papers. For the cops, their legal status was "vagrant." Which is why they all ended up sooner or later in La Santé prison. We lived in the streets, in the cafés, like a pack of mongrel dogs. We had our hierarchy, our very own codes. Students and people with jobs were kept out. As for the few tourists who came around to gawk at "existentialists," it was all right to con them. We always managed to have rough wine and hash from Algeria. We shared everything.
VALI MEYERS

VALI
PHOTO: ED VAN DER ELSKEN / THE NETHERLANDS PHOTO ARCHIVES

The survivors washed up at Moineau's.

That's it. And then it got really crazy. Alcohol, hash—we smoked hash on a regular basis. Nowadays everybody smokes hash. Five million people smoke. In the neighborhood back then hardly anybody did. The stuff arrived courtesy of a fellow called Feuillette, a Moroccan by extraction, who had a connection and dealt in a small way. Also via people like Midou (Mohammed) Dahou, who was a member of the Letterist International, and his brother—they were our guitarists. They were the ones who gave us a rhythmic guitar accompaniment as we were getting blitzed—and they also had hash.

In France it was the Algerians who had hash. They were the only people who smoked it—well, I should say Algerians and Moroccans, North Africans of one kind or another. And we were just a tiny group of people who smoked. Hash then was a very new thing; you could smoke in the street—nobody had the faintest idea what it was.

Where did you buy it?

We used to buy it in Rue Xavier-Privas. The hash would be stuck in disused mailboxes, wrapped in a paper cornet like a portion of fries. There wasn't a single French person down there, apart from us. There were about ten or twelve of us—not just Letterists, but those who were not Letterists were close friends.

You were really the only French habitués of that street and its bars?

Absolutely. There was that street and then there was Rue Galande, which was not so exclusively Arab, a little more mixed, but with two or three strictly Arab bistros. We were the exception. Hanging out with North Africans was a clear way of being against the bourgeoisie, against the morons, against the French. It is hard today to imagine how we experienced the colonial issue back then—it was political, but also visceral. And then after all there was also the Surrealist tradition, Surrealism's great anticolonialist program. It was an elementary thing, and everyone had that attitude, even kids who had never been political.

On 9 April 1950, Easter Sunday of that Holy Year, a small group of people entered the Cathedral of Notre-Dame in Paris, slipped through the large crowd gathered there for High Mass, and approached the altar steps. One of their number, Michel Mourre, wore a Dominican's habit rented the day before for the occasion. The immutable thousand-year-old rite proceeded normally until the moment of the Elevation. It was then that the vast silence blanketing the praying mass was riven by the voice of the false Dominican declaiming as follows:

Today Easter Day of this Holy Year
here
in the exalted Basilica of Notre-Dame of Paris
I accuse
the Universal Catholic Church of the lethal appropriation of our life force in the name of an empty heaven
I accuse
the Catholic Church of swindling
I accuse the Catholic Church of infecting the world with its morality of death
of being a canker on the rotting Western world.
Verily I say unto ye: God is dead.
We spew up from the blandness of your moribund prayers
such rich manure for the killing fields of our Europe.
Go forth into the tragic and elating desert of a land where God is dead and work anew this earth with your bare hands,
with your PROUD hands with your prayerless hands.
Today, Easter Day of this Holy Year here in the exalted Basilica of Notre Dame of France, we proclaim that the Christ-God has died so that man might have everlasting life.

MOHAMMED DAHOU
PHOTO: ED VAN DER ELSKEN/
THE NETHERLANDS PHOTO ARCHIVES

To get back to Moineau's, once you got there, what happened?

Joël and I felt at home there immediately. It was a little bistro that even full to overflowing couldn't fit more than about fifty people—even if the police said 150. The people in Moineau's were wildly different, they had wildly different stories to tell, but almost everyone had the same reaction on first opening the door to the place: the vast majority fled; the rest said to themselves, "Here it is, this is the only place for me!" This group was known to some people as "the family"; my own name for it was "the tribe." Things went on like that for just a little while, not long at all—but such moments are very precious in a life, and distinctly rare.

Who were the first people you met?

There were some I knew already, like Pierre Feuillette and Vali, the Australian redhead, an astonishing girl, visually astonishing, who lived more or less with Feuillette. There were no bar philosophers after the fashion of the Mabillon; they didn't go over there. But there were some people who were slightly more serious, a little more than bar philosophers. Among them was Serge Berna, whom I also knew already. Berna had organized what we called the Notre-Dame scandal with Michel Mourre, then wound up at the Grenier des Maléfices, or Garret of Jinxes, an attic inhabited at one point by a number of neighborhood old-timers; it was on the top floor of an old building (also in Rue Xavier-Privas, by the way, but before we started going there). I know that Ghislain—Ghislain de Marbaix—went there, for one; also the Marshal, a painter who had once belonged to the Surrealist group; Jean-Loup Virmont; Jean-Claude Guilbert,

CHEZ MOINEAU, 22 RUE DU FOUR
STANDING: FRED, MEL, AND A FRIEND OF VALI'S
SITTING, LEFT TO RIGHT: JEAN-MICHEL MENSION, SERGE BERNA, VALI, MICHÈLE BERNSTEIN, JOËL
BERLÉ, PAULETTE VIELHOMME, UNIDENTIFIED GIRL
PHOTO: ED VAN DER ELSKEN / THE NETHERLANDS PHOTO ARCHIVES

Those desirous of engaging more actively in the quest for artificial paradises developed an interest in ether. It was indisputably cheaper than hash, and a rapid effect was assured. No illegal traffic was involved, so no unwelcome police attention was attracted. There were still no restrictions on the sale of ether, and it was readily available from the nearest pharmacist.... When we heard remarks such as "Cap it, Marcel!" we understood that this meant "Marcel, keep your mouth closed—you stink of ether!" When you asked the most seriously hooked whether they planned to continue making *canards*—i.e., dipping sugar lumps in ether—the retort you got was "Don't be silly—we drink it from the bottle!"

Moineau's café in Rue du Four was one of the temples of this ether cult, although not all the Letterists who frequented the place had succumbed to the habit.

For anyone seeking a provisional refuge, if only for a day, Moineau's was the ideal place. This was especially true once the owners of the Mabillon and the Saint-Claude resolved no longer to put up with nonconsumers in their respective establishments. The tourists were coming in droves now, and extras were no longer needed. No such development affected Moineau's, which became the sole safe harbor of circumstance where you could, if need be, sleep for a few hours on a banquette or, when hungry, allay the pangs with a heaping plate of rice or potatoes against a very modest outlay. As refugees from the Mabillon settled in increasing numbers at Moineau's, which had never before known such a crush, there were times when you had to stand waiting for a table. Heretofore the clientele had been almost nonexistent, mainly drinkers of tap water, but now these lonely few seemed to be attracting more serious

whom I'll come back to—they all hung about over there. In short, a few old-timers lived there or went over there because they had no other place—it was a bit like the scene in Renoir's film, *The Lower Depths*. It was there that Berna found a manuscript of Artaud's, *Voyage au Pays des Tarahumaras*, I believe it was. It really was an Artaud manuscript, although at the time everyone treated Serge Berna as a crook—easy enough to do since he was indeed something of a crook! So there were a number of people that I already knew at Moineau's, including a giant of a fellow who used to go to La Pergola sometimes, after returning from Korea (where, incidentally, he had never fired a shot, having been driver to a general). He was an infamous character, very sweet, and would become one of my very closest friends. We called him Fred; his actual name was Auguste Hommel. Later on, he took up painting and supposedly sold well in the United States. He died just recently. What a hulk he was—I called him my "bear." Then there was the old neighborhood gang: Garans, Sacha, Clavel—and Youra, who left later for Brazil; I knew them from the Mabillon, even from the Dupont-Latin. And lots of new faces—people I had never seen anywhere else, belonging mainly to an earlier generation that had experienced the war. I knew them very little. I have named the bistros I used to go to, but there were others in the neighborhood that have now disappeared or gone bankrupt. One was Chez Fraisse, in Rue de Seine, a haunt of Robert Giraud, who was famous for knowing every wine in France. At Moineau's everyone mingled pretty well, except for a hard core of old regulars whom we newcomers obviously pissed off. One of these was Vincente, who had been the bar's "Mother Aub" before our arrival. She thought we smoked too much hash, that we were bringing petty thieves in. The moment came when Joël, Éliane Derumez, and I started taking ether, and naturally we were getting immediately tossed out of every bar we tried to enter, because you could smell the stuff. Old Moineau himself grumbled a bit, but since he was never there in the day, we were able to get in. We very rarely saw Moineau—he only came late in the evening, and even then not every day....

What was he like?

North African, short, pretty typical.... He worked in Les Halles. He had some dough, though. I know that when he opened his bar he gathered people up from the streets, friends of his in the neighborhood, and invited them all in for soup. That's how Moineau's got started. He was a guy who up until then had never had anything to do with Saint-Germain-des-Prés. Old Madame Moineau was French, Breton, I imagine. Well, I say that only because I have known so many Algerian-Breton couples, I may well be wrong. I do know that at one time they had had a café in Rue Dénoyez, in the twentieth arrondissement, at the bottom of Rue de Belleville, an area that was Spanish at the time. There were no North Africans then, not like now, and no Jews, either. There was a tiny Jewish neighborhood across the boulevard, in the eleventh. Anyway, I know that's where their café was. I have a feeling Francis Carco mentions it somewhere. Old Madame Moineau was a woman whom you wouldn't have called beautiful; her nose was slightly hooked, as I remember. I have a photograph.... She used to wear a blue apron—she looked more like a cleaning lady than a café owner.

customers. This hole-in-the-wall of a place, something between a café-cum-coal-merchant and a thieves' den, was being wrenched from its anonymity. The position was still not brilliant, but a glimmer of hope stirred in the heart of Madame Moineau. Little by little she began serving real meals, and ancient aperitifs and spirits were freed at last from their cowls of dust. There was even the occasional slummer bent on a red-wine hangover, and before long Madame Moineau could afford to engage a barmaid. Yet, just as in the darkest days, she could be still be seen lunching, then dining, on a crust of bread dunked in milky coffee.

Moineau's soon became the headquarters of those who later came to be known as "Situationists." Guy Debord, who would soon abandon his second forename, Ernest, was there every day with Michèle Bernstein, today a literary columnist at *Libération*. Also in attendance was my young comrade Jean-Michel Mension, wearing white trousers daubed with variegated printer's letters and Letterist slogans. At Moineau's I sometimes met my friends Gil Wolman and Jean-Louis Brau. There was no shortage of petty pranksters with a hermetic sense of humor, and not a few notorious hoaxes were cooked up on Madame Moineau's banquettes.

A small group that had broken with Isidore Isou called themselves the Letterist International. How could anyone then have imagined that some of their notions foreshadowed the spirit of May 1968, as witness this graffito which appeared on a wall in Rue Mazarine in 1953: "Never Work!" From 1954 to 1957, having left the neighborhood, I more or less regularly received the bulletin of the Letterist International, *Potlatch*. In the meantime, the International had migrated from Moineau's café to Rue de la Montagne-Sainte-Geneviève.

MAURICE RAJSFUS, *Une Enfance laïque et républicaine* (Paris: Manya, 1992)

She ran the bistro?

She was the one that was there all the time, all day long. Moineau only really came in when he'd finished working or before he went to work. We hardly ever saw him.

What about the serving girl?

Her name was Marithé. I found out only later (because at the time I didn't give a shit) that she used to sleep with old Moineau. She was young, really sweet and nice; she lent us money now and then, stood us drinks. On the face of it, you would have expected her to be completely lost, having just arrived from some village. In fact, she had managed to fit in perfectly and adapt to the ambience. And I think she had a few occasional johns in the neighborhood, a few gentlemen friends who would give her a few francs from time to time. But we all got on very well with her. As for old Madame Moineau, she was a saint, she was our mother during that period. She cooked for us. I think her food was awful, actually.

Did she make things easy for you?

Yes, she loved us. Joël, when he pinched things from hotel rooms, would bring them to old Madame Moineau the next morning. At first, she wouldn't want to know about it, then she would relent. She would take an alarm clock against a bottle of wine. She would lecture us, but then.... Once, Éliane and I had skipped out from the Hôtel des Vosges nearby, about three hundred meters from Moineau's, and we had Jean-Claude Guilbert's bags, too, which we had moved out of the hotel two or three days earlier—also a moonlight—about two or

OLD MADAME MOINEAU AND MARITHÉ, THE SERVING GIRL
PHOTO: ED VAN DER ELSKEN / THE NETHERLANDS PHOTO ARCHIVES

JEAN-MICHEL MENSION AND JEAN-CLAUDE GUILBERT (BACK TO CAMERA)
PHOTO: GARANS

three in the afternoon, when the neighborhood was dead. All the bags were tossed out the hotel window and brought over to Moineau's—there must have been ten or so. Éliane and I went off to panhandle, get a few francs together, have a few drinks, and we got back to the bar about an hour later. François Dufrêne had helped with the moving, but he had left. So when we get back to Moineau's, what do we see? Old Madame Moineau chatting as calmly and politely as you please with the lady who owned the hotel, who naturally knew perfectly well that we patronized Moineau's. The two old ladies gave us a talking-to, how it was no way to behave, blah, blah, blah. We swore we'd pay the bill—but, of course, we never did. We couldn't have—it wasn't a question of right and wrong, it was an insurmountable practical problem. Yes, she adored us, that old lady. At the same time she must have hoped that we'd come to our senses, and that no ill would befall us first. She really loved us a lot—we were like her grandchildren.

So despite the drinking, the hashish, the ether, you were tolerated at Moineau's.

Yes, yes—except for the ether. The fact is, though, that if old Moineau, when he came in as he sometimes did around midnight, had made too much of a fuss, everybody would have scrammed. We would simply have found another Moineau's. So he didn't say too much. With the ether, it wasn't so much that it was a drug, more that it smelled bad. Or so they said—we couldn't know. You can drink ether, you know. I never drank it neat, but at one point, when we used to go to Belleville, to my house, in the daytime when my parents weren't there, we used to make ether cocktails.

What were they like?

There were always bottles of liquor at my parents'—they'd sit there for years, because my people weren't drinkers; the liquor was for guests. We used to mix whatever was left in those bottles, add a little ether, and drink the whole thing down.

JEAN-MICHEL AND FRED
PHOTO: ED VAN DER ELSKEN/
THE NETHERLANDS PHOTO ARCHIVES

The life of the Situationist International cannot be disentangled from Saint-Germain-des-Prés and the climate that once reigned in that neighborhood. The Letterist International had set up its headquarters at Moineau's, a low dive in Rue du Four where the Letterists were joined by hitherto unaffiliated young revolutionaries. Drugs, alcohol, and girls (especially underage girls) were part of the folklore of the Letterist International, as revealed in certain slogans of that time which, curiously enough, reappeared on the walls of Paris in May 1968: "Never work!" "Ether is freely available," or "Let us live!"
ÉLIANE BRAU, *Le Situationnisme ou la nouvelle internationale* (Paris: Nouvelles Éditions Debresse, 1968)

You still ended up the night going home to your parents?

There was a whole period during which I would go home to my parents' place at dawn. All things considered, I imagine they preferred that to my being in jail. I had my key, I let myself in, grabbed whatever there was to eat, and left before they got back home.

It wasn't contempt for the family that motivated you, then?

No, no. I had a pressing need for freedom, and I seized the opportunity.

Did you feel you had found that freedom by landing up at Moineau's?

Without a doubt. I had found a kind of family—one very different from the family in the narrow sense, because everybody was a member of it. Not everybody, I mean, but most of the people at Moineau's were friends. This one or that one would have the odd bugbear, naturally, but nothing serious. And then before long I found myself belonging to the Letterist International.

Did you know the Letterist International people before you got to Moineau's?

Not the Letterist International, no. I knew Isou, I knew about Letterism. I knew they produced Letterist poems, because I had definitely been to Isou's recitals at Le Tabou, things of that sort.

JACQUES HERBUTE, KNOWN AS BARATIN, IN FRONT OF MOINEAU'S
PHOTO: ED VAN DER ELSKEN / THE NETHERLANDS PHOTO ARCHIVES

PIERRE FEUILLETTE AND GUY DEBORD ON
BOULEVARD SAINT-MICHEL

And who were the first Letterists you started talking to in Moineau's?

The first, I think, was Guy—except for Berna, whom I knew from before. Anyway, even though he signed the founding document of the LI, Berna never took part in the group's activity. As a guy well known in the neighborhood, he was useful. In a similar way, there were many people around Isou who were not Letterists at all. Everything worked in terms of informal groups, not organizations.

You didn't discuss anything before joining the LI?

Yes, I'm sure we did. But, look, I was ready from the get-go. Ten seconds after Guy mentioned it to me, I was in agreement. If the idea was to stir the shit, of course I was in agreement. No problem there. The first day I spent with Guy that I can remember clearly was 24 September 1952, the day I celebrated my eighteenth birthday. Reaching eighteen was very important to me because it was the penal majority, meaning that from eighteen on you could no longer be sent to a reform school, you could only be sent to prison. You knew that you were going to prison for one month, three months, ten years, whatever it was. With reform school there was what was called the "twenty-one" rule, because, if I'm not mistaken, imprisonment before the age of twenty-one had been abolished at the Liberation. First, you would be in an observation center, and then if you misbehaved you would go up another rung, until step by step you found yourself staying inside for a very long time indeed, without ever knowing when you were getting out. That was what was sinister about it—you were not charged and found guilty of a specific act, instead you were treated as a deviant, as a slightly bizarre creature; it was as though you were expected to straighten up on every count. Reformatories were straightening-up establishments, as their name indeed implies, although that is the opposite of the reason they were set up. What they really did was make a social issue of the "crime" of being young. But when I reached eighteen I became a normal guy who could go to prison just like everyone else.

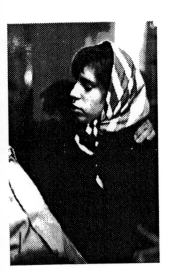

And where did you celebrate that birthday?

My birthday party was on the sidewalk across the boulevard from the Mabillon. I rather think the metro station there was closed at the time. I was drinking—drinking *vin ordinaire* on the sidewalk with Debord. Other people came along; I was panhandling, and so were they. Not Debord—but then Debord had money; he got living expenses from his family, because officially he was a student. People with allowances—there were surprisingly many of them—made it possible for the rest of us who were flat broke to survive. That was another difference: the habitués of the Mabillon didn't dare panhandle, whereas quite a few jokers from Moineau's had concluded that it was a perfectly acceptable means of subsistence.

I can't say too much about my eighteenth birthday, though, because I ended up dead drunk. But I do recall that we stayed there across from the Mabillon for hours, with everyone coming by to shake hands, have a drink with us, or give us a couple of francs. I must have been on that sidewalk most of the day, drinking from the bottle—I was drinking red, I think, and Guy white. That's right, I had red, so he must have had white. I don't know where I ended the day, I don't know whether I finished up at the police station that night or not, whether they arrested me or not. I haven't the slightest recollection.

But that was the beginning of your friendship with Debord?

That was the beginning of our friendship; we sealed it that day, so to speak. After that we went drinking together every day or almost every day for several months. We would go drinking, just the two of us,

Guy with his bottle and I with mine. He was usually the one to pay; occasionally I had money, but as a rule he bought, then we would go to Cour de Rohan, a little courtyard off Rue de l'Ancienne-Comédie, and settle down in the passageway—there are some steps there, and we would sit on the bottom step, holding forth. In other words, we would set the whole world to rights while polishing off a liter or perhaps two liters of wine. That was our aperitif, in a manner of speaking, before we went over to Moineau's.

So you solved the world's problems, did you, in those conversations?

We pulled the world apart and put it back together again—and I imagine there was more of the former than of the latter. Still, it was fairly important work: they were real discussions. Guy, for his part, was highly cultivated, enormously well read. I was rebellion incarnate, and I guess that was what interested Guy—that and my stay in the reformatory; and then, too, the fact that apart from representing revolt I was different from most of the neighborhood people, for whom artistic creation counted for nothing, had no place in their universe....

Was Debord fascinated by people on the lam from society?

On the lam in one way or another, yes. Fascinated, though, not always. Some people came from different backgrounds, or had different histories, went to prison for other reasons. He had a particular fascination with young people, like me, or like Éliane, whom he lived with for a spell. Well, "lived with" is not quite right—it was complicated. Éliane later became Éliane Brau, after having been Éliane Mension. Yes, I think Debord was somewhat

Si vous vous croyez

DU GENIE

ou si vous estimez posséder seulement

UNE INTELLIGENCE BRILLANTE

adressez-vous à l'Internationale lettriste

édité par l'I. L. 32, rue de la montagne-geneviève, paris 5°

If you believe you have

GENIUS

or if you think you have only

A BRILLIANT INTELLIGENCE

write the letterist Internationale

the L. I. 32, rue de la montagne-geneviève, paris 5°

LETTERIST INTERNATIONAL MINIPOSTERS

fascinated by the reformatory or, more precisely, by prison: he thought it was right, it was normal, to go to prison if you led that type of life....

What did you get out of those conversations on the steps in Cour de Rohan?

I had the impression that I saw things a little more clearly; above all, that I was dealing with someone who had ideas about the best way to destroy the world that surrounded us. I was in a primitive state, but Guy had started, I wouldn't say to theorize, exactly, but, well, he would never have signed "General Strike"; he signed things just as violent, but more elaborate. In a way, with us, it was one hand washing the other. This was really the first time I had met a guy who gave me the feeling he was beginning to answer the questions I had been asking myself about a world that was not my world, either East or West, either the Stalinist side or the bourgeois side. And an answer had to be found. Or rather, you weren't obliged to find an answer, you could live without a reply, you could live just for alcohol and dope; of course, that was possible; but I wasn't made that way and I wanted solutions. It was on that basis that I began talking with Guy, and he opened a door for me essentially because I was no longer asking those questions all by myself. Until then the neighborhood had offered a total rebellion, not on everyone's part but on the part of a goodly number of the guys that were there, of the girls that were there: a thoroughgoing revolt that lasted a longer or shorter period of time, depending on the person. But with Guy there was the search for an answer, the will to go beyond revolt, and that was what was exciting to me. It also gave me a chance to go more deeply into what had shaken me up so much in my reading. I discovered that one could try

GIL J WOLMAN AND JEAN-LOUIS BRAU
TRANSFER BY JEAN-LOUIS BRAU
PHOTO: GALERIE 1900–2000

to find solutions in a rotten world. Which is not to say that we proposed to live in that world: at that time we didn't think in terms of living or not living. We didn't think of suicide, either. I used to drink like a fish, so did the others, but we were not suicidal: it was more self-destructiveness. I don't know whether the distinction is clear, but we truly didn't ask ourselves such questions. I don't think people commit suicide, really: I think they try to commit suicide, and those who really try to kill themselves succeed, but in most cases it's baloney. There's something there, of course: people don't behave like that by chance. Guy helped me not to plunge immediately into the depths. Not to become an alcoholic, a full-time gigolo, a thief, whatever you like. He helped me remain somewhat in the world of ideas and not follow the same path as, say, Joël. I am not sure that I would have done so in any case— I'm not gifted in that department—but, thanks to Guy, I used my brain. Thanks to Guy, Gil, and also Jean-Louis, at that time. Guy was useful to me in the sense that because of him I kept a grip on reality—a grip on dreams, too, as strange as that sounds. Dreams are also a kind of reality.

GUY-ERNEST DEBORD

What was your perception of Debord the man?

The impression I retain of Guy is that, in fact, he liked me and that we were also pals, not necessarily the case with everyone.... True, it impressed him that I had been in the reformatory, but it also interested him. I was a youngster who had done things that he was incapable of doing. In a way, I was the existential principle and he was the theoretician; he must have been searching in me for the kind of trigger that causes someone to snap one day and begin living without rules. He himself had never done that: he was still thinking, still exploring, and for a few months there I supplied Guy with something of a point of reference for what youth revolt could be like. Youth revolt was very much an in thing just then. For example, the Marc,O and Dufrêne group, another splinter of the Letterists, were publishing *Le Soulèvement de la Jeunesse* [Youth Rising Up]. So, yes, I was a model, but Guy had others to choose from. No doubt he chose me because I also had a thinking, bookish, intellectual side to me. This was true of Ivan Chtcheglov, too—far more than me, in fact. Guy didn't take as models people who were bound to crack up or people who went too far. He had relationships with such people, but more as bodyguards, guys who stood for force, for organized crime, so to speak—like Ghislain, for instance. Between me and Guy there was no relationship of domination, because I didn't give a flying fuck. And I was perfectly aware, it was obvious, that he knew more than me, had read tons of things that I hadn't read—things he told me all about. So I learned a lot, which got me out of having to read and out of regretting having quit school. Guy taught me stuff on thinkers, on thought, and I taught him stuff about practice, action. He needed to know what he was doing—not me. Here was one guy who was intelligent, an explorer, a seeker, and another fellow—me, as it happened—who after his fashion completely rejected the world we lived in; that was the real connection between us. In a word, we were hell-bent on blowing that world to smithereens together—Guy was the perfect partner for that.

One gets the feeling that as he went along Debord had encounters that allowed him to change course and that he then went on to the next stage, to another sphere. Would you agree with that?

CLAUDE STRELKOFF, KAKI, ÉLIANE DERUMEZ, JOËL BERLÉ, PIERRE FEUILLETTE, GARANS (BACK TO CAMERA)
PHOTO: ED VAN DER ELSKEN / THE NETHERLANDS PHOTO ARCHIVES

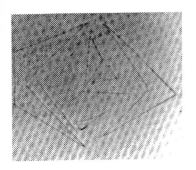

There was something of that. I would not go so far as to say that he took the best people had to offer and incorporated it into his own system, but, yes, there was something of that. There's nothing reprehensible in that, though—quite the contrary. Guy had a lot of finesse, he had great psychological judgment. From one angle, he was very amiable—that was Guy, too. But, of course, he was always goal-oriented, and he was like that because he was on a quest. There was another side to Guy, too, a certain courage: he was always prepared to break off relations even though he didn't always know what he would find next. He took the risk of finding himself alone. And he was always very strict about it: he never maintained a contact when he no longer cared to, except for minor utilitarian reasons. I never understood, for example, why he kept a moron like Conord around; perhaps he found him amusing, and it's true Conord was practical.... I can see it perfectly well with Midou: Midou was a really good comrade who had nothing to do with literature, didn't give a hoot about it, a buddy of Guy's, and he naturally had a role in the group. It would be hard to say that Guy was a man of action, but his thinking was a form of action—he had no wish to become trapped in a soliloquy. He had an aim in life that was a little better defined than ours. We had an aim all right, a very general aim, which was to overthrow the world as it was and then put our heads together as to what we might put in its place. Guy, at least, had a vision of *how* the world might be changed. We others remained at a rather primary level. I myself did have a notion about the eighth art, about the transcendence of art: I believed that the only real art was life itself. I believed this before I knew Guy— it was another reason why we ever met.

So you and Debord would see each other in the daytime, go drinking, go to the cafés, have discussions....

Late afternoon as a rule, because usually I got up late; he got up much earlier. He was living in a hotel in Rue Racine; I have no idea at all what he did in the mornings. He had a more or less regular life in terms of the hours he kept: he never went home really late. During the whole time I knew Guy, I used to get home in the morning five minutes after my mother left for work. He would call it a night fairly early, around midnight or one; he rarely closed Moineau's, and I suppose he must have been in the habit of leaving when he felt he'd reached his limit, had enough to drink. He was methodical that way. He must have drunk alone before I met him about six or so. I never saw Debord dead drunk. I remember a few occasions when he got close, but he never took that fatal glass that would have put him over the edge, whereas for me fatal glasses were the rule.

Did you ever visit him in Rue Racine?

Once or twice. I was quite taken aback to find him in the role of a gent in a dressing gown, very conventional, very bourgeois, you know, the maroon robe with the cord and all that. I thought, "Well, that's odd," but I never pursued it any further.

Most of your time was given over to drinking, then?

Yes, we even held contests. All you had to do was take a small beer glass and fill it, not with beer, but with Negrita rum. So you'd have a glass containing twenty-five centiliters of rum and you had to down it in one go. It was natural selection—well, not so natural, come to think of it.

JEAN-MICHEL AND FRED
PHOTO: ED VAN DER ELSKEN/
THE NETHERLANDS PHOTO ARCHIVES

PIERRE FEUILLETTE AND FRED
PHOTO: ED VAN DER ELSKEN / THE NETHERLANDS PHOTO ARCHIVES

How many contestants at the start?

There weren't a whole lot, because everybody was a bit scared. As winners, there were five, including Guy, me, of course, Joël, I think, and two other clowns—big Fred and Feuillette, if memory serves.

And how many glasses of rum did you have to drink?

Just one, and if you managed to drink it in one draft you would become a member of the—well, of the real tipplers.

The brotherhood?

No, we certainly didn't like that word—I almost said it myself, but it wasn't that exactly.

But there was a little of that?

True, but there was also an element of trying to kill yourself more quickly: we used to drink bottles of wine in one go, liters of beer—they were called *formidables*—in one go, too. We had a pretty remarkable capacity—tolerance, I suppose it was.

Maybe some of us began drinking as a copycat thing. After all, some people get into politics because they make love to a member of the Communist Party. But to take people individually, Guy began drinking before I knew him, very young; Brau likewise started drinking very young, before I knew him; Guilbert started drinking very young, in '44 or '45. Then we joined forces. We were all drinkers already. Well, maybe not all, but certainly those I've named. And Joël started drinking—he was already drinking when I met him. At Moineau's were people who drank seriously. It was one of the reasons people went there. Those who didn't drink

GIL J WOLMAN

never came to Moineau's, they stayed over at the Mabillon. We were always at Moineau's, and we were broke. You would arrive, and there'd be five people at the table saying, "How much dough have you got?" You'd check your pockets and say, "Fifty francs." At the time a hand-drawn liter of wine cost eighty francs. A table of seven might order a bottle, then empty it into the seven glasses—according to each person's thirst, mind you. As soon as someone else arrived the ritual would be repeated.

Guy always drank in an amazing way, taking little sips from morning till night. You didn't notice him drinking, the result being that it was hard to say that he was in an alcoholic state. But he was stewed. One day a fellow started punching Guy out, and he had drunk so much that he was incapable of defending himself. We took turns going outside to give the attacker some of his own medicine. I remember Jean-Claude coming back in saying, "I gave him a good whack," things like that. Then Tonio gets to his feet. "OK, I'm going out there," he says; when he gets back, he goes, "I think he's bleeding a little," and so on.

Brau was one person who at a very young age was completely alcoholic. When he collected his pay or whatever it was, his pension from who knows where, we would practically drink it all up in a night. When Fonta sold a painting, he would usually come by Moineau's, then a few of us would tie one on and emerge only at dawn. Events of this sort were frequent, so there were many days of complete drunkenness. There were times, too, when there wasn't much to drink—no more, say, than a bottle per hour. Alcohol flowed in a perpetual stream, but there were stones in that stream, it was a stream that dried up somewhat according to the hour of the day. For myself, I drank because I couldn't live without it. It was simple, nothing to do with good or bad intentions: to survive, to go on living, I had to have hash and alcohol.

What else did you do at Moineau's aside from drinking?

We used to sing at Moineau's. We sang a lot, we played chess, we talked books, we fell out over ... let me tell you the story of the game of truth, a wonderful story. The game of truth was a big fad at the time among the mandarins, among fancy people in general. The game would end very badly because you ask questions and everyone must respond with the absolute truth. You would hear that such and such a painter had broken off relations with some other painter because the second one had slept with the first one's daughter.... In other words, the game was wreaking havoc in grownup society, and one day someone said, "Hey, let's play the game of truth here at Moineau's." So we sat down and played the game of truth. Of course, it wasn't along the lines of, "Say, Paul, have you ever slept with Françoise?" "Why, yes, as you well know," etc., etc. Because there was nothing to say, nothing at all: everyone knew everything. So very quickly the game broke up amidst monstrous bickering: "I always thought you had Trotskyist tendencies!" "It's time you got rid of your stupid Bukharinism!" It soon turned into a grand talking shop: "Fundamentally you still have an attachment to Surrealism!" "Well, you are still a little tempted by the Communist Party!" "Once a Trotskyite, always a Trotskyite!" Moineau's was such a free place that no one really had any secrets from anyone else. The only thing our game of truth could produce was "You unreconstructed Surrealist!" and the like. It was truly a fine moment.

How did you come to meet the other Letterists?

Gil and Jean-Louis I met a few days after Guy, because he introduced me to them. It was the very beginning of the Letterist periodical, *Internationale Lettriste*. They came to Moineau's, we drank, we smoked hash, and from one day to the next they became my friends. Our coming together found concrete expression in the second issue of *Internationale Lettriste,* just a small mimeographed paper. I was the first new member of the group, but the others already had a shared history. Debord, Wolman, and Brau were the original three. This trio plus Berna made up the foursome who founded the Letterist International, and I was the first to join after that.

The founding trio already had ideas. They had split off from the original Letterists in what might be described as a leftward direction, and if they didn't have a program exactly, they certainly had something clearly thought out in their heads. The other, "historic" Letterists—Isou, Pomerand, and Lemaître—were slightly older and distinctly more oriented toward poetic and artistic activity. The break had occurred in November 1952, in connec-tion with the leaflet against Chaplin signed by Debord, Berna, Brau, and Wolman, from which Isou, Pomerand, and Lemaître disassociated themselves.

Wasn't the Letterist International founded at Aubervilliers?

Officially, yes. I didn't go. I knew the Letterists already, but I didn't go for a very simple reason: intoxication, severe intoxication, added to the fact that I had been picked up in company with another friend, Patrick Straram—who also signed a number

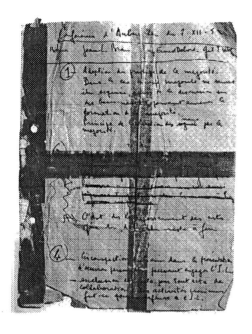

PROTOCOL OF THE AUBERVILLIERS CONFERENCE (7 DECEMBER 1952)

of LI texts, by the way, and who later went to Canada. There he became a sort of guru of the avant-garde, wearing a feather on his head and adopting an Indian name, Bison Ravi. Before leaving France, he wrote a book that was turned down everywhere, a book that in fact recounted an evening at Moineau's, a night at Moineau's, and a *dérive* all the way from Moineau's to the nearest bistro. It was never published, which is a pity, because it is the finest account of the neighborhood as it was at that time. I recall that I played a small part in the narrative: all I said was "OK, Nero," but I said it at regular intervals. Anyway, Guilbert was in it, and the whole gang at Moineau's was described with, I think, great talent; it was very well done, an

excellent portrayal of life then, with its continual excesses.

Straram drank like a fish. He was always getting into tight spots because he didn't hold his drink well, and he would do really stupid things. Several times he wound up in a cell, even in the mental hospital. Once he spent a fortnight there and didn't want to come out. Another time he had a skinful of absinthe someone had brought back from Spain; since he was still a minor and had already been in trouble, he was very afraid of his mom and dad. Not surprising when you think about it—he still had a maid's room in Rue de la Tour in the sixteenth arrondissement. He was on Avenue de l'Opéra threatening passersby with a knife, saying, "Tell me the way to such and such a street or I'll kill you." Naturally, the cops appeared and asked, "What's the idea, young fellow?" And he denied and kept on denying—it was really crazy—that he had drunk more than a glass. The authorities concluded that he was insane and locked him up in Ville-Évrard. It was Totor the Drunk, so called because he didn't drink much at all, who managed to get him out of there. As a matter of fact, his real name wasn't Totor, either; it was Renaud. Renaud wanted to be a psychiatrist. But it was a real job getting Patrick out of that bin. All that trouble for nothing: if only he had said in the first place, "I've drunk half a bottle of absinthe," he would simply have been arrested for public drunkenness and delivered directly to Monsieur and Madame Straram's, where, of course, he would have been in deep doo-doo again.

To get back to Aubervilliers, what the guys told me when they got back was that they had thrown a bottle in the sea—meaning the Aubervilliers Canal—containing the founding document of the LI. Gil, Jean-Louis, and Guy were definitely there, but I can't guarantee that Berna was. In any case,

Berna was pretty much outside the LI. He was the oldest of old-timers in the neighborhood, and his reputation was founded on that—quite rightly.

Berna was older than you?

Yes, he must have belonged to the generation of '25–'26, people who remembered the heyday—which I didn't—of the cigarette traffic at the Liberation, with the Americans and everything. Berna was a pretty brilliant guy.

Did you know others who had been involved in the cigarette traffic?

JEAN-CLAUDE GUILBERT PLAYING ARSÈNE IN ROBERT BRESSON'S *MOUCHETTE*

There was Jean-Claude Guilbert, born in '26—a real character, to say the least. He had arrived in the neighborhood with a Surrealist poet whose name escapes me—a young guy, who wrote for a time, took up painting, and then committed suicide. The two of them lived in Rue de Crimée, but Guilbert's

chief destination when he arrived in Paris was Pigalle, which he soon found to be a fairly dangerous place. He had been a professional gambler, and he was barred, like many professional gamblers, from the casinos. Very few last long in that line, unless they are true geniuses. Anyway, Guilbert had made his living like that for a time, following ship's captains in Rouen: he was very young at the time and had a remarkable capacity for alcohol (which he never lost, by the way), and his job was to get those captains drunk; meanwhile, the guys would be carting off crates of cigarettes and liquor.... In short, he had had a pretty lively youth. After attending Lycée Corneille, he landed in the neighborhood. He was still somewhat serious, however. He had a job of sorts. When we met him he was officially head of personnel in a small TV factory, but he was urging the girls who worked there to strike, so he didn't stay there long! Little by little he became like us. He had all the right qualities for it. He had an immense intelligence and completely rejected society. I wouldn't say that he was a more powerful figure than Guy, but it would be a close call. He always refused to acknowledge his own intellectual capacity: he worked for years in the country—at Bonnieux in the Vaucluse and in Belle-Île, in various different parts over a period of years. He worked as a mason, among other things—he worked continually in a desperate attempt to make people think he had really become something other than an intellectual. Of course, nobody ever believed this. There was one short episode in his life that was a little different: he had bumped into Jacques Kebadian, Bresson's assistant director, and Kebadian got him to do some film acting. He has an important role in *Balthazar*, also in *Mouchette*. Apart from that, he was a mythical drinker. I remember one day he got out of the police station and showed up at Chez

Georges. He promptly asked for one glass of every single drink in the bar. There must have been thirty different kinds of liquor behind that bar, and he drank the lot. Guy would never have pulled a stunt like that; it was pure Guilbert-style alcoholic madness. When I met Guilbert, in '52, he was receiving an allowance from his parents, a small one, but enough to survive on. We would drink it up the first night, or at least we would drink up what little was left of it after outstanding debts had been covered. The morning after not a sou would be left of Guilbert's allowance, the same thing the next month and the same thing the month after that. He used to hang out at Moineau's, but he was never part of the group.

When Debord kicked us out, Éliane and I found ourselves back at Moineau's, and I became closer to Jean-Claude. I wouldn't say that we became buddies—it was something else, not a teacher, either—but he was one of the only guys, maybe the only guy, whose advice I ever listened to, the only guy who I felt knew better than I did about some things. His advice was very functional, very practical. He wasn't the one who told me, "Never admit anything"—that was my mother when I was very small—but he gave me advice about how to deal with society: never cave in, always refuse, never let yourself be had, hold out to the end. In his own way—quite different from my way or Guy's—he did hold out to the end. He never caved in: he was always an absolute thorn in the flesh to society. In the words-that-kill department, he was the champion along with Guy—in those days he was even better at it than Guy. Once, when he was in La Santé, he wrote a letter to the prison director asking for a fork on the grounds that in view of the size of his jaws he was unable to eat with a spoon. It was a brilliant letter—people used to ask Jean-Claude for

advice on letter writing. Debord wasn't then known so much for his wicked pen. He was nice when he wrote—except, of course, for the texts against Isou, but even they were literary, so to speak, rather than insulting. No doubt he caught up later, with a vengeance. You could say, in the end, that Moineau's wasn't big enough for two intelligences like Guy's and Jean-Claude Guilbert's, so one of them had to go. In any case, Jean-Claude's path was a purely individual one. He could never have done what Guy was doing. Success for Jean-Claude was success at doing nothing.

You say there wasn't room enough room for two such intelligences at Moineau's. I've heard something similar said of Hundertwasser, the Austrian painter, who also passed through Moineau's.

Quite possible. There were characters like that; several passed through the café. Hundertwasser himself we rejected the day Michèle Bernstein brought him by in his woolen hat. He failed the entrance test. It was a pretty closed world in there, and there was a selection process that was arbitrary in the extreme. But I don't recall much about Hundertwasser. I have clearer memories of Fuchs, the other painter who became famous later, and the little lady he lived with. Fuchs was something of a crank, something of a mystic, who smoked hash, I think, but wasn't part of the gang. We used to see the two of them, and two or three times at most we found ourselves together on the banquette. But Fuchs was in Moineau's on a fairly regular basis at one point; we knew more or less that he painted, because he or his girlfriend always had a cardboard box containing drawings, sketches. A bit reminiscent of German Romanticism. Or Hieronymus Bosch. I don't really know what became of him afterward; I'd see his name in the paper from time to time.... The pair of them were neighborhood figures, absolutely part of the scene. Though perhaps they drank less than us.

Getting back to Guilbert, did you stay in touch with him?

His whole life, yes. I went and lived with him in the Vaucluse at one stage. I kept up contact when he was in Belle-Île—he stayed there for a few years—and it was me who found his body....

What were the circumstances?

He had cancer of the larynx. Naturally, he refused to get it treated, and he died in his bed. He lived in the ninth arrondissement, in a rather pretty little street; there was a big courtyard, an old barracks I think....

You found him when you went to pay him a visit?

Every Tuesday, in principle, there was a lunch meeting of neighborhood veterans, and one Tuesday Jean-Claude didn't show up. I telephoned, and he told me he was feeling tired. I went by his place the next day, but nobody came to the door. The next day after that I said to my girlfriend, "Listen, we'd better go over there." Still no answer at the door. We called the firemen, and they went in through the window. I found him just in his shirt lying on the bed, dead. So, there it was, we buried him. That was in '91.

How did Jean-Claude Guilbert feel about the old days?

He still had fond feelings for Debord and Wolman—enormously fond. He was still buddies

At Moineau's I got to know some friends of Dufrêne's who at that time were no longer on good terms with him, having had differences of opinion. But the first person to take me there was Jean-Michel Mension. I had met him at Café de la Pergola by the Mabillon metro station. I was seated next to an enormous girl, who must have weighed at least three hundred kilos, and Jean-Michel Mension and a friend of his came over to say hello, because they knew her. Jean-Michel had a drink with us, and it was after that that I began going to Moineau's with him.

During vacation I was working on the abstract film with Villeglé at Saint-Servan when a letter arrived from Jean-Michel informing us that he had met a very charming person named Guy Debord. Debord knew Wolman and Brau because they had all been in the Letterist movement together, before breaking with Isou.

As for Serge Berna, whom we mentioned earlier, he was also a regular at Moineau's, but I knew him from much earlier, from the time of my arrival in Paris, when he was encouraging Michel Mourre to precipitate the "Notre-Dame scandal." While Dufrene and Marc,O were organizing their Youth Rising Up movement, Debord, Brau, and Berna were founding their dissident Letterist International, destined a few years later to become one of the components of the Situationist International.

INTERVIEW OF RAYMOND HAINS BY AUDE BODET (PARIS, 3 MAY 1988)

Such young Letterists as Gil J Wolman and Jean-Louis Brau had met at the young poets group of the Communists' National Writers' Committee (CNE), then under the decrepit thumb of Elsa Triolet.

An anecdote sums up the atmosphere that reigned at the CNE. In the great drawing room, in a most bourgeois manner, each poet would recite in turn, leaning against a monumental fireplace. Seated in a circle, the audience would then grade the poem on a scale of 1 to 10, all the while scrutinizing Elsa Triolet's features to see whether a low or a high mark was desired. Madeleine Riffaud would then take up the scores and calculate the averages, and the most highly rated poems would be published the Friday following in *Les Lettres Françaises*. During one of these sessions, Jean-Louis Brau read a poem of no great interest, in the Dadaist manner, on workers' struggle. Disdainfully Triolet remarked, "Il aime Artaud": "He likes Artaud." Some of her toadies heard this as "Il est marteau"—"He is cracked"—and hastened to pile on with, "Why, yes, he's completely insane," and so on, to the point where a general brawl broke out!

Play in this [Letterist] sense is closely akin to what Wolman calls smoke and mirrors [*fumisterie*]: "With Wolman, you never know whether it is art or filth. Don't wait for him to sit down at the table. I know him. He is likely to cloud the issue. He is a confusionist. The thought that steers the mind forward does not partake of reason, but is all smoke and mirrors. Self-transcendence (smoke and mirrors) springs from all creative works." (Gil J Wolman) ÉLIANE BRAU, *Le Situationnisme ou la nouvelle internationale* (Paris: Nouvelles Éditions Debresse, 1968)

with Sach Strelkoff. He loved Raymond Hains for his clowning, his wordplay, his way of talking about art. He had very good memories of those days, of old Serge, of the old gang and everything.

What of Raymond Hains?

Hains was a character who didn't exactly belong to the group but whom we saw quite often. He was less voluble than he is today, but he talked a fair amount all the same. Always out of time, out of this world, on his own planet....

I worked on a film of his, called *Pénélope*—needless to say, it was never completed. It consisted of pictures of Raymond Hains. If I'm not mistaken, he used a "hypnagogoscope," which was simply a camera with a fluted lens instead of a clear one, which systematically distorted the image. He had it mounted on a kind of rail. He had knocked the thing together himself, and it produced blotches that were continually changing. Éliane and Spacagna—another member of the tribe whom I'd met about the same time as Dufrêne—were the ones who acted as in-betweeners, like the people who draw for animated films. And I would do the developing in a little darkroom. Jacques de la Villeglé was there, too, of course—he used to work with Hains. This went on for several months: we were trying to make a film but could never get it finished. That was impossible with Hains, in any case, so it was hardly important.

A few years ago, Hains had a retrospective at Beaubourg—I think it was two years late opening. The museum management lent him a little flat in Rue Quincampoix, just behind Beaubourg on the corner of Rue de Venise. The place also served as a studio while the exhibition was being prepared. Well, Hains stayed in that flat for far more than two years: first the exhibition was delayed and that gave him an extra year, and then he stayed on for six months after the show closed, supposedly overseeing the move. After the six months, his friends moved all his stuff out and put it in Brancusi's former studio. And when the Brancusi place was fixed up, apparently some works of Hains's were thrown out.

And it was at Hains's place that I began my relationship with Éliane—sometimes we slept on thousands, even millions of francs. We used to spend the night there often—there were two beds. La Villeglé, Hains's big buddy at the time, would be there, and other people would come by. Hains would be in one bed, Jacques in the other, so we would often end up on the floor, but not so much on the floor as on top of a thick layer of torn posters. Considering the price those posters fetched a few years afterward (not quite so much now, I hear), well, you would have to say we were sleeping on a fortune—and it did us no harm at all!

At that time, and in the same café, you got to know Gil J Wolman.

Gil was reticent, sweet—an incredibly sweet guy. I don't think I ever heard him really raise his voice, except occasionally, except when he was reciting his poetry, but that was different. Everyone loved Gil. Here's a story. Once we lived for ten days or so on an enormous fixed-up barge in the port of Paris; actually, I think it was near the Alexander III bridge. This girl, a friend of ours, was supposed to mind the thing while the owner was away. Before long there were fifty or a hundred of us aboard that barge. Obviously, we had to elect people to run things, and limit the, you know.... Well, Gil was elected God. As for me, I was Cabin Boy, and Guilbert, as was only fitting, was Captain.

JACQUES DE LA VILLEGLÉ
PHOTO: BARATIN

EVERTHING THAT IS ROUND IS WOLMAN

I stayed at Gil's for a while, Jean-Louis, too, by the way; we had no places of our own. I can't remember how Gil's mother's house was designed, exactly, but anyway there was a service stairway that was no longer used, and his mother had her studio. Gil had mattresses for us laid out on the landing, and we slept there frequently, and he would bring us our breakfast in the morning....

You were at his parents'?

At his mother's. She was in the garment business, over by Rue Saint-Denis. Gil's father died as a deportee.

Gil led a perfectly normal life?

That's right.

But Gil was not normal at all?

No, he was a genius, in my opinion. And it's not normal to be a genius.

So there were paradoxes about him?

Yes, yes, there certainly were, but I found that out only by getting to know him a little. I knew that with his sidekick, Jean-Louis Brau—and they made a strange couple with Gil so perfectly normal in terms of ordinary life, and Jean-Louis such an obsessive, such a crazy man, you name it—anyway, the two of them had been in Elsa Triolet's National Writers' Committee, then left it and, still together, joined up with the Letterists. They were really very, very close. They went to Algeria together, they met Senac....

What did they do in Algeria?

I don't know exactly, I think they wanted to hitch-hike across the Sahara, and when it didn't work out they stopped part way over. Gil came back, and Jean-Louis stayed on down there for a while.

I am back!... Where were things when you left? Joël has been out for a long time, on probation. Jean-Michel and Fred are now free, too (for stealing from parked cars—and under the influence, naturally). Little Éliane got out of police custody last week after a dramatic arrest in a maid's room somewhere in Vincennes with Joël and Jean-Michel; they were drunk, needless to say, and refused to open up to the police, who left and came back with reinforcements. In the confusion they lost the seal of the Letterist International. Linda not sentenced yet. Sarah still in the reformatory—but her sister, sixteen and a half, has taken her place. There have been other arrests, for narcotics, for who knows what else. It's getting very tiresome. There is G.-E., who has just spent ten days in a nursing home where his parents sent him following a failed attempt to gas himself. He's back in the neighborhood now. Serge is due out on 12 May. The day before yesterday I threw up royally at Moineau's.
The latest diversion in the neighborhood is spending the night in the Catacombs—another of Joël's bright ideas. I have a good many projects which are liable to remain just that—projects....
GIL J WOLMAN TO JEAN-LOUIS BRAU IN THE SAHARA (20 JULY 1953)

FRANÇOIS DUFRÊNE

Originally, Jean-Louis and his people were from Orléansville in Algeria, so, even if he wasn't exactly at home down there—on the contrary, he was a dirty *pied-noir*—at least he knew his way around. Gil, as I said, was one for the quiet life. Not that this prevented him from drinking, though he wasn't perhaps an enormous drinker—he was fairly careful—nor from smoking dope. One night we were all together in a hotel somewhere near Rue du Vieux-Colombier, and Gil spent practically the entire time talking nonsense, at least we could make no sense out of it, and scratching at the carpet—that's how stoned he was. But he did it so sweetly, so calmly.

Still, it was around then, wasn't it, that he made The Anticoncept *and did his* mégapneumies ?

Yes, he was still doing *mégapneumies*. He did two shows, I believe, at Le Tabou.

What was it like at Le Tabou?

I never knew Le Tabou very well—that was the previous generation. I did go now and then, because we ended up there, just as we might have ended up in some other spot. There was jazz there, it must be said. And twice I took part in events at Le Tabou. We had generally drunk a bit beforehand. It was Gil who led the dance. Guy never engaged in actual Letterism, he was never an actual Letterist, so it fell to Gil to start up with his onomatopoeias, his own things, then we would pick up on that, improvise.... I remember one of Wolman's themes: "Op tic tic op op tic tic op"—it was called "47.5 Degrees" or "41.7 Degrees," I don't know which now, but something like that.

But we did it just for fun. We would leave Moineau's, perhaps a dozen of us, and head over there.

What was the ambience like? The atmosphere, the reactions?

Gil's *mégapneumies* were very violent, very physical, using voice techniques to rather extraordinary effect. The two real Letterists were, first, Gil, with a technique that went beyond words, shouting and all that, and then Dufrêne, whose *cris-rhythmes* were more in the line of Artaud. They were the two poets. Unfortunately, Dufrêne was dubbed the Éluard of Letterism, which was tough on him because Éluard was a rat. They were really two great poets—in fact, two great artists. Jean-Louis produced a few Letterist poems, too, but not many—Jean-Louis was pretty much of an idler.

Éliane, who had been Debord's girlfriend, then became your wife, then the wife of Jean-Louis Brau, played an important part throughout those years.

Éliane was a rebel. The daughter of a Hungarian émigré who came to France before the war and who was a glazier and mirror-cutter. Her mother died rather young, of a cancer. She was Spanish. So Éliane was a Hungarian-Spanish mixture, and sometimes it was explosive. Her father had remarried, to a very stupid lady, the housekeeper of a Romanian general who fled Romania after the war, when the country became (or so I am told) a people's democracy. This lady ended up in France, but how old Papaï ran into her, I don't know. Her general, with whom she was still connected, had set her up as concierge in a fancy building he had bought near Michel-Ange, in the sixteenth. Éliane's father became the building handyman—he gave up his

I shall never forget an evening event I attended at the Cercle Paul-Valéry with Jean-Louis Brau and Gil Wolman. The topic that night was the parallel development of music and poetry. A weighty question debated by a group of goateed gentlemen only too aware of the significance of the issue before them. The tedium in that tearoom on Boulevard Saint-Germain was overwhelming, until, with the permission of the master of ceremonies, Gil Wolman, who presented himself as an avant-garde poet, offered his "megapneumatic poetry" to the appreciation of the company. Immediately, Gil hurled in their faces, as you might spit out a stream of insults, a combination of shouts and fevered oaths entitled "Forty-one Degrees and Five-tenths." The disjointed verbal avalanche stunned these amateurs of modern poetry. Some ostentatiously stuck their fingers in their ears by way of protest. The windowpanes of the place were rattling so much that the manager felt the need to close the doors so as not to disturb the neighbors. It was a summer night, and the trying heat conspired with the racket to drive us to the brink of physical confrontation. The good people there must have taken us for escapees from the Sainte-Anne asylum. The evening ended in scandal, amidst flying insults and broken glasses littering the floor. We withdrew in glory, hurried along by the waiters.... I was certainly not committed to this kind of "literature," but the provocations of the Letterists I found most refreshing.
MAURICE RAJSFUS, *Une Enfance laïque et républicaine* (Paris: Manya, 1992)

ÉLIANE
PHOTO: ED VAN DER ELSKEN / THE NETHERLANDS PHOTO ARCHIVES

mirror cutting. A handyman in that part of Paris could do better than a qualified mirror-cutter in the eleventh. Éliane had grown up in a little neighborhood not far from the town hall of the eleventh arrondissement, not far from Place Léon-Blum (the vile Léon Blum)—a very working-class neighborhood. She couldn't stand this woman who had nothing to say, absolutely nothing to say, so she walked out; her father went down to the nearest police station, as usual, and when the cops caught up with Éliane she was sent to a reformatory in Chevilly-Larue. Her father wanted to take her home, but the cops said, "No, no, it doesn't work like that: you came in and reported her, so...." Anyway, I think she escaped a first time from Chevilly, then she was picked up again. Later she left that reformatory—it wasn't a reformatory, exactly; there was a real warren of houses of correction, of this and that, waiting for you when you got out; in principle you stayed at Chevilly-Larue for three months, then you went to a harder place, or else to what was called a "Bon-Pasteur," a place run by nuns. Éliane ended up in a Bon-Pasteur, in the sixteenth, I think, and she was supposed to take courses outside, typing, secretarial—the classic women's jobs. She didn't go to her classes much, though—instead, she would come down to the neighborhood to smoke a little hash; she loved hash, and we used to smoke a lot of it. Inevitably, she absconded from her Bon-Pasteur and had the cops on her tail again. I say the cops—specifically, it was the Juvenile Squad, whose chief at that time was Commissioner Marchand, the best-known policeman in all the neighborhood bars. So Guy must have met Éliane at the time when—or just before she escaped from that Bon-Pasteur place.

In 1953–54, at Rue Delambre, our visitors got to see how for five hours each day a two-rooms-with-kitchen, a Second Empire rent-machine, could be transformed into a film studio. There would be Jean-Michel spelling Raymond in the darkroom; Éliane Papaï, in-betweener of the moment, at the focusing screen; and Jacques Spacagna in the painting room spreading oil-based paint over the cards and cels. In a corner, the "Hypnagogoscope" awaited the shots being prepared.
VILLEGLÉ, *Urbi et orbi*
(Paris: Editions W, 1986)

So at the time she was still answerable to the juvenile authorities?

That's right. I got to know her a short while before she ran away, and then when she ran away, she and Guy broke up and she and I started living together. When she came to the neighborhood and smoked, we didn't stay there. I often went with her under a bridge—for the longest time I believed that that bridge was the Pont de Sully, whereas in fact it was the next one along. For forty years of my life, or almost, I had those two bridges mixed up! Hardly important, I suppose. One day Éliane and I went back to Raymond Hains's place in Rue Delambre and made love, just as almost everyone used to.... I thought for years that she had parted from Guy in that same casual way. Only recently did I learn that Guy had a very, very pure vision of eternal love, perfect love, a vision impossible to live out in this lousy world, and that, in fact, they had split up over a word, a chance remark, that tended to contradict that view of things. Neither Éliane nor Guy were in the wrong—it was a case of, you know, the boat of everyday life....

So you and Éliane got married?

I got married to Éliane because she was still on the run from the Juvenile Squad. It was in late '53; she was just under eighteen. Majority for penal purposes was eighteen, but as a fugitive she was still under the jurisdiction of the Ministry of Justice and the Juvenile Squad. That was the whole beauty of the marriage idea. In any case, minors are never treated as people in the full sense. We were liable to arrest from one day—or rather from one night—to the next. So I went to my mother and said, "Listen, I have to talk to you..."—

and I told her the facts just as they were. My mother replied, "Good, that's fine"—well, that's a bit of an exaggeration; what she said was, "If that's how it is, all right," and I imagine that in the back of her mind was the idea that if I got married to Éliane I might at long last come to my senses. So it was my mother who did the sweet-talking to Éliane's father, who in fact didn't have a clue what was going on, and we were legally married. My mother got me a suit for the occasion—the only time in her life she did such a thing, thank goodness! She bought it from the old Jewish part of the family—or what little was left of it after the deportations—at Kremlin-Bicêtre. As for Éliane, she had people lend her some spiffy clothes. Then we got married. There were the two witnesses, my parents, her parents.... Afterward, we went straight back to the neighborhood, Éliane changed, and we continued drinking at Moineau's.

RAYMOND HAINS AT HOME, RUE
DELAMBRE, PARIS
PHOTO: HARRY SHUNK

Éliane was already something of a drinker, was she?

Yes. At the start she didn't drink much, she smoked hash, mostly. Soon she started drinking because everybody else drank. You couldn't stay in that bar and not drink. At twelve-thirty or one in the morning we left Moineau's and went over to settle some outstanding business with the owner of the Mabillon, who a few days earlier had called the cops on Éliane. The help locked the café doors, and the boss came out to palaver. Éliane insulted him. I must have done the same. At some point Éliane asked me what to do next, and I said to her very agreeably, "Kick him in the balls, for good measure"—which she proceeded to do without hesitation. The guy went back inside his bistro; then while we were still standing on the sidewalk just in front of the café people came up to us and offered their congratulations. We never did know whether they were congratulating us because Éliane had kicked the café owner in the balls, which would have been eminently courteous of them, or because we had been married, which would have been the height of idiocy. Next, we had to stop two passing bicycle cops ourselves in order to get escorted to the Saint-Germain police station in Rue de l'Abbaye. When we got there I tossed our new family identification document on the counter and said, "Leave my wife alone. Éliane Papaï no longer exists!" Then I went into a ghastly song and dance—so ghastly that the police had it in for us for ages afterward. I feel we had a valid excuse for getting married—we weren't doing it just for an extra franc or two from social security. So, anyway, we spent our wedding night in the police station. In principle, I am against marriage. We would never have got married if it weren't for Éliane's problems. A few days later we went to try and sell our wedding rings to an old jeweler lady in Rue du Four, but she told us that the rings were quite worthless—just the cheap old silver commonly used for such rings. In any case, we had got them from a jeweler and watchmaker who monitored the banns posted in the municipal offices and then offered rings free to all the future newlyweds. Naturally, ninety percent of the people who received the rings bought other things—silver spoons, knives, and so on. We didn't want to buy anything, so we finished up with our two rings, and seeing how little selling them was going to get us to drink, we decided to keep them. We preferred panhandling to selling them.

Was Éliane merely a rebel? Wasn't she almost wild?

She was wild, yes, even mean, horrible—she was a scandal. She was just fine and, I would say, magnificent. After I came back from Algeria at the end of '57, in contrast to the earlier period, we used to go to bars on the Right Bank, and I remember at least two of them where Éliane stripped her clothes off and started dancing on the table at one in the morning. The customers loved it, even though as she danced, half Spanish, half Gypsy, and half drunk, she was knocking their drinks onto the floor. They were as happy as could be. That was typical Éliane, always causing something of a scandal. Sometimes she would have a cleanliness crisis and start washing her panties out in the gutter....

Here's a good Éliane story. Often, around two in the morning, when Moineau's closed, we would take the same short route via little Rue des Ciseaux to the Saint-Claude, which was on Boulevard Saint-Germain. By tradition, we would take a piss en route in a corner where everybody used to piss. One night, just to give us a bad time, the cops came down on us: wham-bang! drunk and disorderly! They knew the lot of us. Your papers, please, the whole shebang—not excluding Éliane, who had pissed along with everyone else and who was now shouting: "Not on your life! I would never piss in front of guys!" In a word, she was putting on a great show. Her cop was pretty good-humored, and he didn't give a damn what she was on about. Then Éliane goes: "Look, I can prove that I didn't piss." She pulls down her panties, squats, and starts pissing all over again in front of the cop. So the cop slaps her with another ticket. I reckon it must be a world record—a women's world record, anyway: two summonses for drunk and disorderly conduct in the space of fifteen minutes.

So she had great timing and she loved to provoke.

Oh, yes. She was an absolute menace whenever we landed in the police station. Which was very often. There was a time when we were regularly being run down there two or three times a week. There were three police stations: Rue de l'Abbaye, Place Saint-Sulpice, and Rue Jean-Bart. We would go to one or another of them according to their rotations. There were nights when we paid visits to all three. Éliane's great specialty was clinging to the bars of the holding cage they had in the station. At first we wouldn't be put in cells, but confined in that tiny space; Éliane would clamp herself onto the bars, screaming "Jacot! Jacot!" and she would go on for a very long time indeed. After a while the cops would toss us into the cells, but in the meantime Éliane was completely insufferable. That's what I loved about her: she was whole and entire. That's what we all loved, in fact—Guy, Jean-Louis, and I. I think we all had the same vision of Éliane. In Debord's *Oeuvres Cinématographiques Complètes* [Complete Cinematographic Works] there is a fantastic photo of her: it shows all the hate in the world, all the fear in the world, all the violence, all the refusal ... she was truly a great lady. I no longer had any recollection of this portrait, and when I opened the book and came upon it ... it was a poignant moment for me.

LA FRANCE SEULE

possède un bar comme **L'HOMME DE MAIN**
31, rue de Jussieu

"FRANCE ALONE HAS A BAR LIKE L'HOMME DE MAIN [THE HIRED THUG]"
SMALL POSTER DESIGNED BY GUY DEBORD FOR THE OPENING OF GHISLAIN
DESNOYERS DE MARBAIX'S BAR

*So that was the tribe—Debord, Wolman, those who were
so to speak "legal," and then you, Joël Berlé, Éliane
Papaï, who were perhaps in a way more marginal?*

Éliane, not so much—it was just that she had left
home....

*But she was continually getting into trouble with the
police, wasn't she?*

Yes. She also took part in our wine pilfering, things
like that. Once, with Joël and Éliane, we got ourselves arrested in Pépère's flat in Vincennes. Pépère
was a guy who had been in the penal colony at
Cayenne—I think he had been accused of murder,
of killing a prison guard. His voice was almost
inaudible, he used to mumble incomprehensibly in
the slang of Cayenne. His family, who must have
had some money, tried to have him live decently,
honestly. That was how he came to have some
brand-new shirts, which we were trying to barter for
bottles of wine. And that's why the cops came looking for us—they thought we had stolen the shirts. In
the fistfight that followed we lost the seal of the
Letterist International. I know that later Pépère
died a stupid death near the Church of La
Madeleine: he was panhandling, I suppose he was
sitting on the ground, when a political gunfight
broke out between rival Algerian nationalists, FLN
versus MNA, and Pépère took a stray bullet. Joël got
much further into crime than we ever did. We were
never anything but petty thieves; we never committed many crimes.... Berna went to jail even after he
was in the LI, also for stealing, I think. He was sent
to the prison of Draguignon, where he wrote a very
fine song:

Quand vient chanson
douce lueur
à la lisière de ma douleur
pauvre pauvre bateleur
l'hiver s'en ira sonnant l'heure
du renouveau sans ton bonheur
pauvre pauvre bateleur

When song brings
its tender glow
to the edge of my pain
poor, poor buffoon
winter will depart tolling the hour
of renewal without your happiness
poor, poor buffoon

MAX BOULINIER, ORGAN
BUILDER, KNOWN AS
THE CARDINAL

At one time, we used to sing that song often at Moineau's. So it's true, Berna was a bit of a crook, a bit of a thief, but he was very intelligent—very cunning, too. He had a sort of genius for entertaining scams, for thinking up schemes....

What of Ghislain de Marbaix?

Ghislain de Marbaix was not really a Moineau person, but he was a neighborhood person. I met him first at the Mabillon. He was in fact an elder, a big brain of the neighborhood, and a brute of a man physically, incredibly powerful, especially when he had been drinking. The legend was that he once broke a guy's arm in an arm-wrestling match. There were others who claimed that he had once punched a man to death; but I imagine he himself put that story about. He was a real force of nature. He was also a pimp. When we knew him he was with a girl we called "the Antillaise," the West Indian, who had a baby. He would drop by Moineau's now and again. He had a big mouth, and a very common way of

speaking despite the noble origins indicated by his name, Ghislain de Marbaix of something or other that I forget. He was a character, with a very special way of expressing himself, an enormous beard, an imposing body. He was part of the decor. I think he eventually became very pally with Debord. They liked each other well enough at Moineau's; they would chat, but it was later on that they got onto quite intimate terms, meaning they would see each other frequently and continually. We couldn't have cared less whether he was a pimp or not, but we never really knew because he was rather secretive. Ghislain was someone we liked a lot, because he was so much less pretentious and idiotic than some of the jokers playing the philosopher in the Mabillon. Ghislain was someone who already had his feet firmly on the ground, and he was dangerous when drunk; you really had to watch your step then. As I say, he got very friendly with Guy some time after my departure. In a way, he played the same part as Hafid or Midou earlier: something of a bodyguard to Guy. I'm sure Guy also liked him because he was an adventurer, a complete original. I went several times to his bar, L'Homme de Main, for which Guy designed a little poster, but it was the sort of bar that functions mainly at night, and I would never get there sober. It was a dive, pretty dark inside. Marise would be there, whom I got to know much better later on; she's the one Guy calls "La Tatouée" in his memoirs: a rather extraordinary young lady who used to prostitute herself over by Rue Vignon, near La Madeleine. I am not at all sure that Ghislain pressured her in the slightest to do so. It is quite possible that she chose that way of life herself. In any case they lived together for a while; then later, at the time of the bar, things fell apart. The last time I went over there, I don't remember seeing Ghislain; I remember Marise and fat Fred, that's all. Ghislain disappeared, and then one day we learned that he had got himself blown away. Because he really was a goon. He belonged to the underworld, though I don't know exactly what he used to do. Apparently, he had been a bodyguard to a number of people mixed up in politics, Gaullist politics—Service Action Civique (SAC), no doubt, De Gaulle's political police—that sort of area.

Michel Smolianoff, known as "Nonosse," was another one of us, something like Fred in general type. He had a fabulous voice, an extraordinary deep voice that you could hear from three kilometers away. At the time of the famous Meeting of Failures, Nonosse was a sandwich man wandering up and down the Boul' Mich' advertising the event and its program. Among the participants was the fellow we used to call "the Cardinal," and the Marshal was also definitely in the picture. The Meeting of Failures took place just as I was arriving in the neighborhood—I was still at the Dupont-Latin. I was still going home to my parents' place every night, so I couldn't attend, but it was one of the things that made a great impression on me.

SERGE BERNA AND JACQUES MOREAU, AKA THE MARSHAL

Was Berna there?

Yes, in fact, I'm sure it was Berna who cooked the thing up. Along with a few of his Letterist pals. You might say they were the crème de la crème of the neighborhood—the failed of the failed. They had written a leaflet called "Ratés" [Failures] that said: "They portray us as DUDS, and that is what we are. We are nothing, we mean it, NOTHING AT ALL, and we intend to be of NO USE."

R A T É S ....

On nous présente comme des ZÉROS, et nous le sommes.

Nous ne sommes rien, mais alors là, RIEN du TOUT,

et nous entendons ne servir à RIEN.

.es "honnêtes gens" nous rabâchent : "TRAVAILLEZ ! MAIS ARRIVEZ DONC !!

ARRIVER OÙ ? ARRIVER A QUOI ? ET DANS QUEL ÉTAT ?

otre devise : POUR ARRIVER, SURTOUT NE PAS PARTIR.

   INCAPABLES
      INUTILES
         OISIFS
            VA-NU-PIEDS de COMPTOIRS !

Venez vous reconnaître et vous affirmer

au

GRAND MEETING DES RATÉS

qui se tiendra en l'hôtel des Sociétés Savantes

8, Rue Serpente, Paris (5°)

le 16 Mars 1950 à 20 H.15

- - - - - - - - - - - - - - - -

Disserteront : "Des mérites de l'Impuissance"

Serge BERNA : syphilitique de gauche

Maurice-Paul COLTE : individu

Jacques PATRY : ancien Dominicain

Buffet gratuit
       ainsi que
           Madeleine AUERBACH

LEAFLET ANNOUNCING THE MEETING OF FAILURES

How did the meeting go?

There must have been different contributions, including one by Berna. I remember that there was a "left-wing syphilitic." It was all about creating organized scandal and also, of course, a way of relieving the suckers, the tourists, of their money—because everything revolved somewhat around that, too. We weren't all crooks—Berna was, yes—but we had to live, and at the same time we weren't supposed to work. You were an idiot if you got a job; it was simply not done in those days—you lost respect.

But when you announce that you are good-for-nothings, aren't you really thinking that you are everything?

Yes, of course—it's very, very pretentious. But, on the other hand, it was true—we really were good-for-nothings. We were good for living in that world of ours; in their world we were good for nothing, but in ours, which naturally we considered infinitely superior, the situation was entirely different.

You wanted to live outside the economy?

No, we never put things in such terms. Much later, Debord dealt with Marxism at length, he read it all, but in my time we never discussed Marx. Brau certainly knew a bit, considering his family background: his father must have been a member of the Communist Party, because he was deputy mayor of Aubervilliers in Charles Tillion's time. Jean-Louis professed a certain knowledge, therefore, and he had certainly read Marx's writings, but I personally never talked about Marx with either Gil or Guy.

FAILURES....
They portray us as DUDS, and that is what we are.
We are nothing, we mean it,
NOTHING AT ALL, and we intend to be of NO USE.
"Respectable people" harp on:
"WORK! BUCK UP! SUCCEED!"
SUCCEED IN GETTING WHERE?
IN DOING WHAT? IN WHAT CONDITION?
Our motto: IN ORDER TO ARRIVE, ABOVE ALL, *DO NOT LEAVE*.
All you INCAPABLE, USELESS, IDLE, RAGGEDY BARFLIES!
Come and acknowledge one another and assert yourselves at the
GRAND MEETING OF FAILURES to be held at the House of Learned Societies, 8 Rue Serpente, Paris 5.
15 March 1950. 8:15 p.m.
The following will discuss "The Merits of Impotence":
Sege BERNA, left-wing syphilitic
Maurice-Paul COUTE, individual
Jacques PATRY, former Dominican
A free buffet will be served along with Madeleine AUERBACH.
Evening dress required!

GIL WOLMAN AND ISIDORE ISOU

The relationship between Gil and Guy was a relationship between creators. Guy was the theoretician of so-called political thought, Gil the theoretician of "dispainting," as I think he called it; that is to say, the theoretician of artistic noncreation, of how to proceed after painting has been transcended, how to carry on when painting no longer serves any purpose. One was the political aspect, the other the artistic aspect of the will to connect politics and art and meld them into a whole. I think Wolman, in Guy's eyes, was a truly extraordinary artist, clearly superior to the other artists in the Letterist International. Personally, I've never believed in the exclusion of Gil. You know his formula as well as I do: "One does not exclude the other." Quite obviously, Debord was obliged to call Gil's departure an exclusion, but I believe it was really far more of a separation.

Gil lived his own life. He always had a family life, a perfectly conventional life on one side, something that never failed slightly to surprise everyone, because, after all, the rest of us were not exactly conventional. At the same time, he had an astonishing creative ability that at least to my mind surpassed that of any other artist of his time. Anyway, the two aspects came together. Granted, that's not the way Guy tells it: naturally, he could not allow himself to say that anyone left without so much as a by-your-leave. The same goes for Ivan Chtcheglov, who ended up in the loony bin. Gil and Ivan were both people who had a big impact initially on Guy's thinking, people who helped him develop his projects. Later came Asger Jorn, and others.... At all events, Guy had a special respect for Gil. They were on truly very good terms. So were Guy and Jean-

Louis at the beginning, at Moineau's—everything was just fine until Jean-Louis started up with his military nonsense.

Which was what, exactly?

I think Jean-Louis enlisted—I can't remember whether it was for Indochina or Algeria. In short, I believe he was excluded by Guy for militarism, and quite rightly so. Subsequently, he led a rather strange life, traveling a great deal, doing all kinds of things.

He was on the list of excludees published in Potlatch *No. 3.*

Yes, but that list is a mixture. On the one hand, you have Isou, Lemaître, and Pomerand, the three Letterists. They weren't excluded at all. Guy says that they were excluded, but in reality it was a schism, a split.... The original Letterists had started long before my arrival on the scene. Maurice Lemaître was the right-hand man of Isou—a scoundrel.

Who was the scoundrel, Isou or Lemaître—or both?

Oh, Lemaître, absolutely. Isou was not a scoundrel, he was a nice guy. In the first place, he was completely mad, but at the same time he was a very serious person—he didn't drink—with his feet firmly on the ground. He was quite convinced, however, of his own genius. Later on, he resented Debord for pinching his position as leader. But that occurred on much more of a political basis than an artistic one. In any event, I feel it would be interesting to extract the avant-garde kernel from Isou's thought: the issue of "externality," the issue of youth revolt, the

KICKED OUT.
Since November 1952, the Letterist International has been proceeding with the elimination of the "Old Guard." A few of the excluded, with reasons:
Isidore Godstein, alias Jean-Isidore Isou: morally retrograde individual with limited ambitions.
Moïse Bismuth, alias Maurice Lemaître: delayed infantilism, dementia praecox, plays the saint.
Pomerans, alias Gabriel Pomerand: fabricator, nullity.
Serge Berna: lack of intellectual rigor.
Mension: merely decorative.
Jean-Louis Brau: militarist deviation.
Langlais: stupidity.
Yvan Chtchegloff, alias Gilles Ivain: mythomania, delusions of interpretation, lack of revolutionary consciousness.
It is useless to revisit the dead. The automatic door closer will take care of them.
GIL J WOLMAN, *Potlatch* No. 2 (29 JUNE 1954)

"Plan for the Reform of Secondary Education. We demand a reduction
in years of study and an authentic reform of secondary education.
By François Dufrêne"
Le Soulèvement de la Jeunesse No. 3 (October 1953)

sense that youth was going to play a different role in the period then beginning—all perceptions that were very much ahead of their time. But I think that as an artist Isou was not very talented; he wasn't a good painter.

So the rotter was Lemaître, whose real name was, I believe, Moïse Bismuth?

I have never been quite certain that he was really called Bismuth. I have often wondered whether it was not in fact Gil, Jean-Louis, and Guy who made the name of Moïse Bismuth up for him. Someone should check. Even when he ran for election as a deputy from the seventeenth arrondissement, he used the name Lemaître. Still, he could have changed his name; people did it some at that time.

They did, certainly, but when you are in an avant-garde milieu, you are defying society by definition, and surely you defy society as what you were from the outset, not masking what you are, not seeking to adopt another identity. Unfortunately, even Isou was really named Goldstein....

Be that as it may, the avant-garde milieu is small, at the time of the Letterists it was extremely small, and obviously everybody knew that Isou was Jewish. He could have called himself Dupont, and they would still have known it. He was Romanian. According to what I was told at the time, he had been a leader of a youth organization close to the Communist Party in Romania; when the freeze came, he got out—a good thing, too—but he had very left-wing connections when he first arrived. We were fond of Isou, we had nothing at all against him, and, furthermore, Guy, Gil, and Brau all had respect for him. We looked upon him as someone who had

made a real contribution. Lemaître was merely Isou's factotum, bodyguard, right-hand man, whatever you want to call it. We didn't like him because—well, because we had to be against someone over there. As for Pomerand, who was, in fact, the third member of the Isou group, we never saw him, he was no longer around; he was off in some other part of the neighborhood, doing other stuff....

You had mentioned François Dufrêne....

At that time Dufrêne and Isou were on the outs. Dufrêne was the enemy because he was involved with Youth Rising Up. This was a fairly political group—more directly political, certainly, than either the LI or Isou's old guard. They were putting out a paper of the same name. They had Marc,O and, I think, two girls: one was Yolande du Luart, the other was Poucette. All this was going on around the time of the split in the French section of the Fourth International. François Dufrêne had been taking some kind of courses; in the Marxist political jargon they were known as training school.

Yes, training schools—the Communist Party had them, too....

Exactly. The Youth Rising Up people were much concerned with the idea of "externality"—the notion that the working class was no longer the center of the universe, that the revolution was not going to depend on the working class. There was a new phenomenon, in the shape of youth, which was external to production, but which was becoming more and more important, etc., etc.

The center of the universe was now the avant-garde?

That's right. As a matter of fact, the famous axiom, "Only the working class is revolutionary to the end," was outdated for the Letterists as a whole. The Youth Rising Up thing set out to mobilize people as militants, but, in fact, it didn't last long, a couple of years, maybe. When I got to know François well, which was in 1954, after my exclusion from the LI, he was already out of Youth Rising Up. I remember that what was left of the group once decided to interview François and me, but we gave such a scandalous interview that they never published it.

Was Dufrêne a drinker, too?

During that period, Dufrêne drank a great deal. Afterward, we hung around a lot together. In '55 we produced a spoken daily news bulletin called *Le Petit Stupéfiant* [The Little Narcotic]. There was Guilbert, François, me, Éliane, and also two or three friends of François's who were not neighborhood people but people whom he had met in the poetry world—pretty serious people, though I must say they, too, took up drinking then for a few months.

Where was this spoken news bulletin produced?

On a bench on Place Saint-Sulpice. We were waiting for Godot, of course, and we did a bit of panhandling. Some of us had a little money. We used to buy hand-drawn wine at Chez Georges in Rue de Canettes, and we drank enormously. That was it. I don't know what we did really, no one knew exactly what was in the news bulletins, but still, we commented on the events of the day. I'm sure Dufrêne must have presented some of his own stuff. We

"Three mental cases? Three louts? Three heroes? This page is intended to let you make up your own mind about the act of Michel Mourre, 21 years of age (the fake Dominican), Serge Bernard [*sic*] and Ghislain Desnoyers de Marbais [*sic*], here shown together on a bench at the Saint-Gervais district police station."
COMBAT (12 APRIL 1950)

After *Traité de Bave et d'Éternité*
[Treatise on Slobber and Eternity],
Isou's cinematographic production dried
up. For one thing, imagination was in
short supply and, for another, working
with film was an expensive business,
even without considering laboratory pro-
cessing and studio costs. Those hitherto
faithful to Isidore Isou began to turn
their backs on him; they wanted to go
beyond their master, no doubt—but how
does one improve on mediocrity? Still, in
1951, Gil Wolman presented
L'Anticoncept [The Anticoncept] also at
the Palais de Chaillot, while Gabriel
Pomerand was making his *La Légende
visible*, using images by Léonore Fini.
As for François Dufrêne, his film *Les
Trompettes du premier jugement*
[Trumpets of the First Judgment]
had dispensed with the classic moving-
picture component altogether and made
do solely with a sound track recounting
the dream images that the filmmaker
would have liked to present. Then came
Guy-Ernest Debord, announcing the
opening of his film *Hurlements en faveur
de Sade* [Howls in Favor of Sade]. It was

even came close to going over to a written newspaper. Uncharacteristically, Guilbert produced the first
few pages, but I lost them. So that was our chief
occupation: we sometimes stayed as long as two or
three hours over on Place Saint-Sulpice preparing
and delivering our news bulletin.

Did you get on well with François Dufrêne?

We adored each other, we hung about together a lot,
we were real bosom buddies. We often used to go
with Éliane to Rue Vercingétorix, where Dufrêne's
father had a studio. There were paintings by the
father—nothing special, he was an occasional
painter—as well as Dufrêne's own pictures and
those of Jean-Philippe Bernigaud, known as Talbot,
François's best friend. Those two were always
together. They had been at the same high school or
the same university, I don't remember which, along
with a certain Maspéro who would make his reputation later in an area very far removed from artistic
creation. As a matter of fact, Bernigaud-Talbot
always remained François Maspéro's right-hand
man at his publishing house, Éditions Maspéro, and
at his famous bookshop, La Joie de Lire.

*What about Marc,O—Marc-Gilbert Guillaumain—
did you know him?*

No, I never knew Marc,O at all. But I remember
him as part of the enemy in Youth Rising Up.

*Was the Youth Rising Up group at the showing of
Hurlements en faveur de Sade [Howls in Favor
of Sade]?*

Yes, at the second showing, at the Ciné-Club du
Quartier Latin, in the Salle des Sociétés Savantes in

Rue Danton. I was not present at the first screening, in June, at the Ciné-Club d'Avant-Garde; at that time I didn't yet know Guy.

This was the time fisticuffs broke out immediately?

No, not immediately. We managed to keep things going for quite a while.

What happened?

We—by which I mean to say the LI—were in the balcony, with our supporters. I was with a girl called Francine. She was in love with a guy who did mime, so I did mime because I was in love with her. And there were other friends from Moineau's, including Gil and Jean-Louis and Jean-Louis's wife, Françoise. On the ground floor were the Youth Rising Up group, with Dufrêne, Marc,O, Yolande du Luart, and another chick. A professor from the Cinémathèque of Lausanne got up on the stage and explained that in the film we were about to see there was an erotic tension that gradually increased, that was all-consuming, that got you by the throat ... in short, he gave a whole long speech. A number of people in the audience recognized him, because it was Serge Berna—a false professor, of course—the same Berna who had committed the Notre-Dame scandal with Michel Mourre and Ghislain de Marbaix shortly before. Disguised as a monk, Mourre had interrupted Easter High Mass by going up to the altar and delivering a sermon violently attacking the Church and including the proclamation, "God is dead!" The three intruders were almost lynched on the spot and wound up in the police station.

to be the cinematographic event of the season, and the Ciné-Club du Quartier Latin had agreed, in the context of its program of avant-garde film, to bring this new breakthrough in Letterist cinema to the public. The Salle des Sociétés Savantes was packed from the orchestra to the balcony, with fifteen or so sardonic-looking Letterists occupying the front rows. I had met with Debord that afternoon, and he had asked me to attend with a few of my friends; the evening promised to be nothing if not tumultuous. I was ever eager for such escapades, and I had no difficulty finding other scandal-lovers to go along with me. At the appointed hour there was a goodly number of us ensconced in the balcony, ready to support our Letterist comrades vocally and, if need be, physically, against the challenges anticipated. Act one. Introduced as a Swiss professor of filmology (*sic*), Serge Berna mounted the dais to present this work of the century: "Ladies and gentlemen, this evening we offer you a profoundly erotic film. Bold in a manner never before seen. A work that will mark a date in the history of the cinema: the time of wine and walnuts. That is all I can reveal to you now, as I don't want to spoil the surprise." Once complete darkness had enveloped the audience, an announcement was made to the effect that the reels had not yet arrived and that there would be a few minutes' delay; the lighting went up to low. After a quarter of an hour, Debord arrived at last with the film canisters under his arm and briskly climbed the few steps to the projection box. Darkness descended once more. The characteristic sound of the projector was heard, and in the darkness, by way of credits, a monotone voice began enumerating a few cardinal dates in the history of the cinema, among them the date of birth of Guy-Ernest Debord, 1932, and the year of creation of *Hurlements en faveur de Sade*, 1952. Then silence. The darkness was total, and only the whirring of the projector was to be heard. Surely images would soon be forthcoming? This was not even a provocation—simply a mild joke. Light filled the screen. During the darkness, silence had reigned. Now murmuring began to be heard in the audience, but the grumbles were quickly overwhelmed by a series of statements on the sound track—extracts, more or less, from the Penal Code. Darkness and silence then resumed for ten minutes or so, after which we were rewarded, as it were, by a desperate voice: "I'll say nothing more without my lawyer present!" Another spell of silence. The joke had now lasted about three-quarters of an hour. Protest began to make serious inroads. Invective started flying in both directions. One Letterist proclaimed, "The eroticism should occur in the audience"—this in reply to a spectator expressing astonishment at the absence of spicy images. The public was billowing forth its resentment at having seen strictly nothing. Nobody could believe that the director would leave his audience—there was an admission fee, after all—without offering them a single image: in the end, no doubt, one would probably get a little something—some kind of provocation, at least. With the uproar gradually gaining ground in the orchestra, the Letterists and their allies in the balcony bombarded the public below with stink bombs and sneezing powder. The better equipped hurled water-filled condoms. Once the munitions ran out, spitballs replaced the projectiles. The last minutes of the film consisted of total darkness. No one had walked out. The show had begun about nine, and at ten-thirty the lights went up definitively to the catcalls of a frenzied public. The master of ceremonies seized on a brief moment of respite to announce question-and-answer time. Ever serious, Serge Berna spoke, developing a few complimentary thoughts concerning Guy-Ernest Debord

What about the rest of the audience?

They were the usual habitués of the Ciné-Club du Quartier Latin, which at the time had a big membership. This was the heyday of film clubs in Paris. Students, young people, neighborhood folks would go simply to see a film ... but, of course, that day plenty of them, not being idiots by nature or by nurture, had an idea of what kind of film was being shown. Anyway, after a time the Dufrêne people started shouting, crying scandal, insulting us. The public followed suit. We responded in kind from the balcony. I remember yelling what I thought was a very clever line from high in the balcony: "You are fakes and we are forgers!" Aside from which, I never did go to bed with the young woman I was with—it was close, though.

Was the film shown to the end?

I don't believe so. Most of it, however. In the end, naturally, the "arousers of youth," who, after all, were fairly intelligent people, fairly clever, managed the not too difficult feat of arousing the audience against us. We got out of there alive, very thirsty, and very pleased.

What occurred after the showing?

We left after the film. We insulted the people, and they insulted us. Then we went drinking. I can't imagine that we could have done anything else. I don't have any recollection of the drink after the showing, but obviously we must have gone back to Moineau's....

I have just reread *Hurlements en faveur de Sade* and discovered that a famous sentence that I remembered so well and carted around in my head

JEAN-MICHEL AND FRED
PHOTO: ED VAN DER ELSKEN / THE NETHERLANDS PHOTO ARCHIVES

JEAN-MICHEL MENSION AND PIERRE FEUILLETTE PLAYING CHESS. CENTER: ÉLIANE
PHOTO: ED VAN DER ELSKEN / THE NETHERLANDS PHOTO ARCHIVES

all my life—"L'Isère et la misère, continue ma petite soeur, nous ne sommes pas beau à voir" [The river Isère and poverty, continues, my little sister, we are not beautiful to see]—simply never existed; it had another form altogether, even if the text says the same thing concerning that little girl who threw herself into the Isère. I always remembered the sentence in that form though, so, of course, I'm not going to change it now, after forty years. In any event, the text of *Hurlements* is very beautiful. I advertised that film by writing its title on the white painter's pants that I was wearing in those days. "Hurlements en faveur de Sade" are the only words that can just be made out on all the photographs I've seen of me in those pants.

Is that why you were excluded from the LI on the grounds that you were "merely decorative"?

That's right. It's true—I was very decorative.

What was your reaction when you learned that...

Oh, it wasn't until much later that I learned that I had been labeled in that way. It amused me, because I was certainly decorative with those white pants spotted with paint and covered with slogans.

I suppose I must have been sad until the next time I tied one on. Two or three days later I was over it. I went back to Moineau's, because by that time, remember, we were no longer in the old neighborhood, we had moved to Rue de la Montagne-Sainte-Geneviève. Back at Moineau's, I rejoined old friends—Guilbert and the other excluded Letterists. Then I got to know François Dufrêne, and a week later it was all over. But I have always regretted being excluded, because I felt that Guy was a person of exceptional intelligence.

and his oeuvre. One spectator, trembling with rage, demanded an explanation of the filmmaker's reasons for entitling his film *Hurlements en faveur de Sade*. Completely straight-faced, Berna responded that there was a misunderstanding and that the film was really dedicated to a friend of Debord's, one Ernest Sade, currently engaged in the worthy trade of procurer in Rue Nicholas-Flamel. With this improvisation of Berna's, the evening was brought to a close amid an indescribable hullabaloo. The Letterists had not wasted their time. The Debord film was worth easily ten films from Isou, and the absence of images was entirely salutary. A voluntary esthetic *dérive* must naturally refrain from imposing on specatators any cinematographic "writing" that could expose it to criticism. If the aim was to make a tabula rasa of the ideas of the past, then what was to be achieved would certainly be found by hewing to this line. Born agitators, some Letterists demonstrated considerable talent as soon as they escaped the influence of their master. Their everyday behavior shed much light in this connection, for these marginals lived their lives in the open, invoking no particular esthetic principles in support of their approach. Though Letterism disappeared as a form of expression, the traces left by Isou's disciples would prove to be indelible until about 1968.
MAURICE RAJSFUS, *Une Enfance laïque et républicaine* (Paris: Manya, 1992)

But how exactly did the break occur?

That's a question I have asked myself many a time. And I have never managed to answer it properly. I imagine things must have fallen apart somewhat, that Debord was a little more dispassionate for a few days. But the fact is that I can't recall the break itself.

And how was it when you found yourselves in the same café?

I recall a time when we happened to be in the Monaco at the same time. Quite a few Americans use to be at the Monaco then, and the way it worked was that everyone would buy a round, except for the Americans. When it was my turn, I didn't pay for Guy, and likewise when it was his round he didn't pay for me. Suppose we were six drinking: I or Guy would pay for five glasses only, and the other would pay for his own separately. It was a ritual: we would not say a word to each other. It never crossed my mind to address him, and the same was true for him. That kind of thing was just not done.

But you continued to relate to other members of the group?

No—it was forbidden, we didn't have the right. Members weren't allowed to keep on talking to the others—to neighborhood people, yes, but to people who had been excluded, that was taboo.

How long did this continue, passing people in the street without saying a word?

Not long at all, because afterward I left for Algeria, where I did a lot of drinking, as per usual. I didn't see Guy in the neighborhood after that, or not more than once or twice. I got news of him, because he would see mutual friends, neighborhood old-timers that he would have a few drinks and get drunk with, who would then tell me things like, "Say, Guy is in such and such a café at the moment." Or, "Guy is over at so and so's." Or, "Guy has gone to Spain." I imagine he got news of former friends likewise, certainly of our old gang from Moineau's, via people he ran into here or there: "Jean-Michel has joined the Party" or "Jean-Michel is a Trostkyist now." He is bound to have heard things like that through normal channels.

And, of course, over time you must have heard much talk of Debord.

I heard talk of Debord when *Potlatch* was being put out. I rather think the idea of *Potlatch* was already a little bit in the air before I left—at any rate, the word "potlatch" had already been found. Afterward, for many years, I didn't keep up at all, absolutely not.

Was the rite of exclusion modeled on Surrealist practices?

As a matter of fact, there was no rite of exclusion. What happened, roughly speaking, was that before starting *Potlatch*, Guy excluded everyone he had known at Moineau's who had been a participant, anyone who had signed texts. This is not to say that he broke off with all of them. He continued seeing Conord, for instance, and Patrick Straram, and even Henry de Béarn, who was a very big pal of Chtcheglov's. But he dismissed practically the entire Moineau team and set off again with a new team which did, however, include Bernstein, who

INTERNATIONALE LETTRISTE N° 4   JUIN 1954

La Guerre de la Liberté doit être faite avec Colère

pour l'Internationale Lettriste :

Henry de Béarn, André-Frank Conord, Mohamed Dahou, Guy-Ernest Debord, Jacques Fillon, Gilles Ivain, Patrick Straram, Gil J Wolman.

"THE WAR FOR FREEDOM MUST BE WAGED WITH ANGER"
INTERNATIONALE LETTRISTE No. 4 (JUNE 1954)

was a Moineau person. It was more a matter of housecleaning than of exclusion, I think, and there was a playful element in it, too. He didn't start afresh from nothing, but he renewed the team completely, while keeping up some relationships, because they were virtually the only ones he had in Paris. Later he formed others, under other circumstances, but at that moment Guy didn't have many connections beyond the Moineau crowd. Anyway, he made a fresh start. Even Ivan was excluded then—though I had always thought that he was excluded much later, at least six months or a year later. Time is quite relative in these matters. It was only when I went back to the texts that I realized he had been excluded very quickly. What's the date of the issue of *Potlatch* with the exclusions?

June '54.

That gives me a better idea, because I really couldn't say for sure myself when exactly Debord and I separated. If that issue is dated June '54, then it must have been in the spring of '54.

Berna was excluded, too.

Yes, he was, but he genuinely didn't give a shit.

Langlais was excluded for "stupidity."

Yes, I think that's right. But I never really cottoned to Gaëtan—I could take him or leave him.

IVAN VLADIMIROVITCH CHTCHEGLOV, AKA GILLES IVAIN
PHOTO: GARANS

But how can I forget the one whom I see everywhere at the high point of our adventures: the one who, in those uncertain days, opened a new road and advanced down it so quickly, choosing those who would come along? For no one else was his equal that year. You would have said that merely by contemplating the city, merely by contemplating life, he changed them. In a single year he raised a century's worth of demands; the depths and the mysteries of urban space were his conquests. GUY DEBORD, *In Girum imus nocte et consumimur igni* (1978)

And with Chtcheglov it was for "mythomania, delusions of interpretation, lack of revolutionary consciousness."

Chtcheglov, well, Guy reversed himself on that later. But lack of revolutionary consciousness—that was true. Chtcheglov was never a revolutionary.

Who was Chtcheglov?

First of all, Ivan Chtcheglov's name brings to mind the famous attack on the Eiffel Tower. The story goes that Chtcheglov and Henry de Béarn used to share digs near the Champ-de-Mars, and that the blinking lights of the Eiffel Tower used to disturb them greatly. They had, therefore, decided to blow up the tower. Of course, everyone knew about their plan and, consequently, so did the cops. One day they left the neighborhood with a haversack—I have no idea what it really contained—intending to blow up the monument, and sure enough they were nabbed before they had gone thirty meters. But when you think about it carefully.... Many a time I've wondered whether it was just the blinking lights that kept them from sleeping, and whether there wasn't something more on Chtcheglov's mind: considering the state in which we generally got home at night (or rather in the morning), even an Eiffel Tower looming above couldn't really have kept anybody awake.

IVAN CHTCHEGLOV
PHOTO: GARANS

Chtcheglov drank, too?

Chtcheglov drank less, I think.

So what was on Chtcheglov's mind apart from the flashing lights that kept him from sleeping?

There was almost all the culture in the world. He was extraordinarily well read. He was fairly young, but he had studied a mass of stuff, he knew a mass of stuff; he came from a family of intellectuals, pretty much. I went two or three times to his home, in the sixteenth, where his old parents lived, completely traditional, completely bourgeois. I don't know quite whether they were White Russians, but they were definitely émigrés from who knows when, an old family, complete with a family grocery where an old lady served us, on credit, if need be. Chtcheglov was a kid who fit comfortably into his family when he wanted to; he was not at odds with his parents. And he was full of ideas. Chtcheglov had a tic: sometimes we would take the metro and

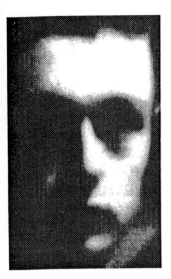

Ivan Chtcheglov

he would keep saying "I have a tic, I have a tic, I have a tic." His tic was to have a tic, to say that he had a tic. It could go on for the whole journey.

What impression did Chtcheglov give at first encounter?

A kind of smile, and the clear sense that he had a strong desire to have everyone on.

And when you got closer to him?

You still felt he was having you on, that he would never take this universe very seriously. Was there a link between this and what happened to him later? I couldn't say. But I must say that I already felt that he was like me, that he didn't belong in this world....

But you still felt different?

Yes. He came from somewhere else.... But, of course, we were all different—at Moineau's there weren't two people who were alike. In any case, Chtcheglov didn't seem any more "crazy" than anyone else in the gang.

What happened with him, exactly?

Whether it was the effects of alcohol, or the effects of himself, he started—along with Gaëtan, by the way—seeing Tibetan lamas all over the place, becoming more like a reader of *Planète*, more Surrealist. That was not the Guy Debord line, which was very specific. So Ivan was excluded. Later on, he married Stella, and then one day when he had been drinking he wrecked an entire bar. Certainly he had behavioral problems, but we don't really know, we can't really know—he was so

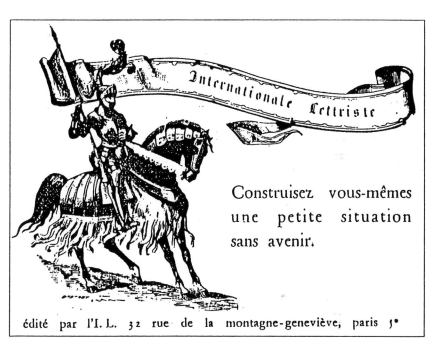

Construisez vous-mêmes une petite situation sans avenir.

édité par l'I. L. 32 rue de la montagne-geneviève, paris 5°

"CREATE YOUR OWN LITTLE SITUATION WITH NO PROSPECTS."
MINIPOSTER OF THE LETTERIST INTERNATIONAL

GARANS, YOURA, CLAUDE CLAVEL, SACHA STRELKOFF
PHOTO: ED VAN DER ELSKEN / THE NETHERLANDS PHOTO ARCHIVES

destroyed at the hospital, what with the insulin and the electroshock treatment, which would obviously have driven even a sane person mad.... Our view at the time was that demolishing a whole billiard room while completely drunk was insufficient justification for calling the cops and having a person forcibly committed. Ivan's girlfriend Stella signed something called a voluntary commitment authorization—in reality, a totally involuntary arrangement—and Ivan found himself in the mental hospital. He was allowed out on leave but would return of his own free will. He was a ruin, albeit a fine ruin, of his former self. He had been defined as schizophrenic. Those were the days of insulin-induced coma and electroshock, and he described these things in splendidly lyrical terms.

CENTER: MICHÈLE BERNSTEIN GIVING A LIGHT TO ÉLIANE, WHO IS SITTING ON HER KNEE. HALF VISIBLE: ANDRÉ-FRANCK CONORD. TO HIS RIGHT: MÉZIANE. FAR LEFT, REFLECTED IN MIRROR: JEAN-LOUIS BRAU. PHOTO: ED VAN DER ELSKEN / THE NETHERLANDS PHOTO ARCHIVES

What were Chtcheglov's relations with Debord like?

Debord and he were extremely close. Debord paid enormous attention to Chtcheglov, enormous. Chtcheglov's ideas were already formed, and I think he helped Guy a great deal in his search, helped him make progress on the issue of urbanism, on the issue of the relationship between art and life. Ivan had ideas that were truly quite personal to him. He was a genuine visionary, I would say, something of that order.

What about the dérive, *how did that get started? You would be wandering the streets, walking....*

The first true *dérives* were in no way distinct from what we did in the ordinary way. We went on walks from time to time. One among others that became traditional took us from the neighborhood to the Chinese section around Rue Chalon—behind the Gare de Lyon. We would eat over there, because it was not expensive, or occasionally we would stop on the way near Saint-Paul to buy salted anchovies, which made us desperately thirsty. Then we would make our way back as best we could. Some made it, some didn't, some collapsed en route. We also used to visit the Spanish neighborhood along the canal at Aubervilliers. We would go there either at the start or at the end of the night. There was chorizo, paella.... Old workers' bistros frequented in the main by guys who had arrived after the Spanish Civil War, Republicans. We were pretty well received, because we drank enormously. But those were the sort of places where we never arrived completely straight and often left dead drunk.

To begin with, then, there was no theorizing about the dérive?

Not at the outset, not really. Chance played a big part. Take the rail strike in the summer of 1953, for instance. That was a very special time: no trains were running, and public transport in Paris was also at a standstill. There was a lot of hitchhiking and military trucks ferrying people about. For a few days, hitching became a perfectly normal way to get around the city. We used to go to the Gare de Lyon to support the strikers and thumb our noses at the people waiting for trains. We couldn't stick around for too long because we would have been set upon. My first *dérives* were with Guy, Éliane, and Éliane's girlfriend, Linda. It was simple: we started hitchhiking, and the fourth or fifth car would pick us up. Guy would buy bottles of wine from a café, we would drink them, then set off hitching again. We went on like that until we were completely potted. Not all that poetic, really. At that time I used to find it very tiring to walk. Naturally, we used to walk around the streets in the neighborhood, and when

JEAN-CLAUDE GUILBERT, ÉLIANE, AND JEAN-MICHEL MENSION
PHOTO: GARANS

POTLATCH POTLATCH POTLATCH POTLATCH POTLATCH POTLATCH POTLATCH POTLAT

potlatch

POTLATCH POTLATCH POTLATCH POTLATCH POTLATCH POTLATCH POTLATCH POTLAT

bulletin d'information du groupe français de l'internationale lettriste
paraît tous les mardis   n°1 - 22 juin 1954

POTLATCH :   Vous le recevrez souvent. L'Internationale lettriste
y traitera des problèmes de la semaine. Potlatch est la publication
la plus engagée du monde: nous travaillons à l'établissement conscient
et collectif d'une nouvelle civilisation.
                                              La Rédaction

TOUTE L'EAU DE LA MER NE POURRAIT PAS...

Le 1er décembre, Marcelle M., âgée de seize ans, tente de se suicider
avec son amant. L'individu, majeur et marié, ose déclarer, après qu'on
les ait sauvés, qu'il a été entraîné "à son corps défendant". Marcelle
est déférée à un tribunal pour enfants qui doit "apprécier sa part de
responsabilité moralé".
En France, les mineures sont enfermées dans des prisons généralement
religieuses. On y fait passer leur jeunesse.

Le 5 février, à Madrid, dix-huit anarchistes qui ont essayé de recons-
tituer la C.N.T. sont condamnés pour rebellion militaire.
Les bénisseurs-fusilleurs de Franco protègent la sinistre "civilisation occidentale".

Les hebdomadaires du mois d'avril publient, pour leur pittoresque,
certaines photos du Kenya: le rebelle "général Chine" entendant sa
sentence de mort. La carlingue d'un avion de la Royal Air Force où
trente-quatre silhouettes peintes représentent autant d'indigènes mi-
traillés au sol.
Un noir abattu s'appelle un Mau-Mau.

Le 1er juin, dans le ridicule "Figaro", Mauriac blâme Françoise Sagan
de ne point prêcher,- à l'heure où l'Empire s'en va en eau de boudin,
- quelques unes des valeurs bien françaises qui nous attachent le peu-
ple marocain par exemple. (Naturellement nous n'avons pas une minute
à perdre pour lire les romans et les romancières de cette petite année
1954, mais quand on ressemble à Mauriac, il est obscène de parler
d'une fille de dix-huit ans.)
Le dernier numéro de la revue néo-surréaliste,- et jusqu'à présent in-
offensive,- "Médium" tourne à la provocation: le fasciste Geoges Sou-
lès surgit au sommaire sous le pseudonyme d'Abellio; Gérard Legrand
s'attaque aux travailleurs nord-africains de Paris.

La peur des vraies questions et la complaisance envers des modes in-
tellectuelles périmées rassemblent ainsi les professionnels de l'écri-
ture, qu'elle se veuille édifiante ou révoltée comme Camus.

Ce qui manque à ces messieurs, c'est la Terreur.
                                              Guy-Ernest Debord

UN NOUVEAU MYTHE
                   Les derniers lamas sont morts, mais Ivich a les yeux
bridés. Qui seront les enfants d'Ivich ?
Dés maintenant Ivich attend, n'importe où dans le monde.
                                              André-Frank Conord

POTLATCH No. 1

we were panhandling, walking was unavoidable. But going to the Chinese area was a heroic expedition, and Aubervilliers was even worse. Don't forget, we were drunk, and distances are greater when you are drunk: you don't walk in a straight line, so....

Then, in late '53, you all moved from Moineau's to Rue de la Montagne-Sainte-Geneviève—which you called "Rue de la Montagne-Geneviève."

That's right—no saints allowed, of course. The move meant that everyone now mingled. I don't know how we landed there, whether Guy had a precise plan. I do know that later on he had a precise plan about the thirteenth arrondissement, which was to undertake *dérives* over there. It was a very old quarter where buildings were already beginning to be demolished, one of the first quarters to feel the brunt of the new urbanism, but still a very interesting corner of the city. It was slated as the first area to be systematically torn down and transformed. Very working class, lots of factories, very Communist Party, very left-wing. There were buildings there— just as there were on the outer boulevards, the Boulevards des Maréchaux—that were practically unassailable. The cops never showed their faces in places like that. There was also Les Halles—but Les Halles was a slightly different case. I really don't know whether our migration, so to speak, from Moineau's to Charlot's on Rue de la Montagne-Sainte-Geneviève was part of Guy's strategy, but I rather doubt that it was pure happenstance.

Twenty-nine numbers of *Potlatch* were published in 27 installments between 22 June 1954 and 5 November 1957 (Nos. 9–11, dated 17–31 August 1954, constituted a triple issue). From No. 1 to No. 21, *Potlatch* was subtitled "Information Bulletin of the French Group of the Letterist International," and then, for the remainder of the series, "Information Bulletin of the Letterist International." Until the said triple issue the paper appeared weekly (on Tuesdays); from No. 12 on, it became a monthly; and from No. 26 on, publication was irregular. The paper's successive editors-in-chief were André-Franck Conord (Nos. 1–8), Mohammed Dahou (Nos. 9–18), Gil J Wolman (No. 19), and Jacques Fillon (Nos. 23–24). Later issues appeared without mention of an editor-in-chief. *Potlatch* was composed of sheets measuring 21 by 31 centimeters with typed text recto and verso, mimeographed. The sheets were stapled together at the upper left corner. The length varied from one to four sheets, and the print count increased over the series from 50 to 500 copies. *Potlatch* was never sold. On 15 July 1959 there appeared the first (and last) number of a "new series" of *Potlatch*, subtitled "Internal Information Bulletin of the Situationist International." (Text: Henri Polaklaan)

Charlot's was the bistro right next to 32 Rue de la Montagne-Sainte-Geneviève, wasn't it?

No, number 32 *was* the bistro: our legal address was Charlot's itself. And that was where we got together, sometimes there and sometimes, for a while, in the old neighborhood. Then one day Guy decided—or we decided, but no doubt at Guy's suggestion—that henceforward we would no longer go to the old neighborhood, and that anyone who did would no longer belong to the group. Still, there were people who came to see us: there was Michèle Bernstein, who at the time was not officially in the group; there were old-timers from Moineau's; Ghislain came a few times; Guilbert would come over and go on a bender....

You say that Michèle Bernstein was not yet a group member. What year was this?

When I first met her at Moineau's in 1952 she used to be in almost every day, but she worked, she was a serious person. I think she was still taking courses and working at the same time. I got to know her about the same time as Guy did, but she was not in the group, nor was she, I believe, in '53. In any case, she didn't sign any LI texts. She signed from the beginning of *Potlatch*, and she joined the group formally at that time. Guy and Michèle were married very soon after, in August '54.

Were you aware of their getting married?

Yes, because Guy's new group was not watertight at the time when I was excluded. A number of friends who had never been part of the old group continued to see Guy and drink with him. There was Sacha, there was Guilbert—the break was not complete.

MICHÈLE BERNSTEIN AND GUY DEBORD ON A BALCONY OF THE HOTEL IN RUE RACINE
PHOTO: JACQUES FILLON

Up until my ill-fated departure for Algeria, in early
'56, I had news of Guy regularly.

*Michèle Bernstein's name appears for the first time just
after your exclusion; namely, in* Potlatch *No. 3, which
came out in July 1954.*

That's it exactly. I remember one afternoon when
we had been drinking together, the three of us. I
told them they were made for each other and, in
effect, that they ought to get married, and indeed I
felt it would be a good idea. Guy was amazingly cultivated, and he had remarkable ideas for the time—
and for later times, too, for that matter; and
Bernstein for her part, though completely different,
had an exceptional classical culture and vast knowledge. To me, and to others at the time, she was a
walking dictionary. She came from a highly cultured
background.

How did the neighborhood people perceive her?

A pain in the rear end. She was seen as an outsider,
because she had a job. She was working part-time,
student jobs....

But her working was useful.

Yes, because she always had a couple of francs on her.

And she stood you drinks with them?

Oh, yes, absolutely. She was really nice. I remember
one morning coming into Moineau's with Joël Berlé,
about eleven, and she was there already, because
she used to eat lunch at Moineau's—the cheapest
bistro in Paris. Right away she started ordering
glasses of red for us. But she was a little different.

She was appealing, and, furthermore, it was very pleasant occasionally to hear her talking of various writers and suchlike. But Michèle had a slight air of sophistication that placed her outside our little family. There was a whiff of "fancy neighborhood" about her. That said, we were very fond of her—she was intolerable, but, as I remember, we were very fond of her.

How did she and Guy respond when you suggested they get married?

They said "Alright"—and Guy had another drink. I can see him now, with his smile that was a little ... a little sly. I don't know if they had already thought of it, if marriage was something they already had in mind. I made the remark in a perfectly natural way—they
seemed to me like an extraordinary match.

Apart from Michèle, who were the girls around you all at that time? Were there many?

At Moineau's there were a few, yes.

Can you be more specific?

Before Éliane, I lived with Sarah Abouaf, who signed several Letterist texts. She lived on the outskirts of Paris, in a hostel for Jewish girls whose parents had died as deportees. I don't know how she ended up in the neighborhood. But, anyway, I leaped at her. and she leaped at me, and that was how she got to Moineau's.

Was she a minor?

Oh, yes—and in fact she got herself caught and sent to a reformatory. Later on, her sister, who was even younger, came by to tell me what had happened when Sarah was up before the judge—and to cut a long story short, the little sister ended up staying in the neighborhood, too. I took her to my old friend Raymond Hains's house, and she replaced her sister among us. She was called Sylvie, I think. Then there were women who passed through, who came and went. Often they came into Moineau's much as they might go into the Mabillon; it depended on which of our crew had picked them up. Some stayed the day, some stayed longer—and some stayed a very long time, indeed. There were other ladies, too, much older, by which I mean they must have been at least twenty-five. You had girls who worked—two in particular, quite extraordinary, who worked at the Hôtel des Impôts, the tax department on Place Saint-Sulpice—and a few ladies who were semiprofessionals, who had a gentleman friend or two, like Marithé, the serving girl. There were even a few really old ladies, one of whom used to wait impatiently in hopes of picking up a drunk at six in the morning and taking him home. Practically everyone at Moineau's fell into her clutches sooner or later—Germaine was her name.

You too?

Yes, but actually there were two of them—I was caught by one but managed to escape the other. We also had the dresser of Louis Jouvet's theater troupe; she had toured with him in Latin America during the war and washed up at Moineau's, who knows how. And a girl who had been a ticket-puncher in the metro. It was one of the gang that brought her in one day. She left her ticket-punching gizmo on the seat when she left. Then she quit her metro job and became a Moineau person.

At all events, I'm sure that, living the life you did, you had a better chance of meeting girls than other boys your age.

Oh, yes, the level of sexual activity must certainly have surpassed the national average. Naturally, we were not faithful, either on principle or by inclination; nobody is faithful by inclination—and we were not faithful on principle, either. It was quite inevitable, therefore, that after a while everybody had spent a tender moment or two with most of the others. Not with all, but everyone had had two, three, four, or five liaisons in succession. All the girls had slept with Feuillette, because Feuillette was public property—it was Feuillette who was easy, not the women. There was also the matter of homosexuality. In the group, old Serge was bisexual, Raymond Hains is homosexual, François and Spacagna also on occasion, Joël, me....

Was it overt?

Yes, at that time it was all part of the game: you were supposed to do everything, try everything. But some of the older people, for example, Guilbert, were not too fond of queers.

Did you try everything yourself?

Yes—well, perhaps not everything, I must have left a few gaps! Don't forget, though, that the others imagined me a sort of Rimbaud at the time; and they had me play that role. There was a Brazilian filmmaker called Orlando who had come to Paris to

ORLANDO
PHOTO: GARANS

JEAN-MICHEL IN HAT, FRED, AND A TOURIST
PHOTO: ED VAN DER ELSKEN / THE NETHERLANDS PHOTO ARCHIVES

make a film but ended up spending several years in Moineau's before going home, and he was in love with me and called me "the archangel." Still, those who looked upon homosexuality as perfectly healthy and normal were a restricted group. In the neighborhood there were people, known as *truqueurs*—fakers—who cruised around looking for homos to entrap and beat up—quite a fashionable sport in those days.

How did you of the tribe view artists?

The first thing we had to say about painters was not very theoretical, because it was, "There's a cocktail party tomorrow evening at such and such a gallery in such and such a street." What painters meant to us was first and foremost a chance to drink and a chance to eat: we tried never to miss an important opening. So the painters' primary function was utilitarian. That said, I don't think we had any theory on the subject, not as I recall. We thought they were nice, we knew a few slightly, but their world was not our world. I remember Dominguez, a tall Spaniard who drank like a fish. We were fond of Fonta, because he also drank like a fish and paid for our drinks. He was a very bad painter, a watercolorist, very bad, an old man from the point of view of painting. I remember Michaux, too, but we were hardly paying attention. We had nothing against painters in general. We had a lot against Surrealists, on the other hand. A case of murder of the father, obviously. We looked upon Surrealists as cops....

What did you all know, at the time, of the Surrealist movement, its history, Breton and the others?

What I knew to begin with—and I was not alone in this—was from the Nadeau book, *The History of*

TOTEM AND TABOO
First shown on 11 February 1952 and immediately banned by the Censorship Office for reasons that remain unclear, Gil J Wolman's first film, *The Anticoncept*, may still not be exhibited, even in noncommercial venues.

This film, which marks a clear turning point, is withheld from the public by a committee made up of heads of household and police brass. When the powers of the cop are added to the professional blindness of the critic, we have idiots banning anything they don't understand.

It is true that *The Anticoncept* is more loaded with explosives for the intelligence than the irritating truck in Clouzot's *Wages of Fear* and more offensive today than the images of Eisenstein, which frightened Europe for so long.

The most overtly threatening aspect of a work such as this, however, is that it contests so absolutely the yardsticks and perishable conventions of those heads of household and police brass; and that it is bound to endure, at the source of the coming troubles, long after these stooge censors have vanished.

GUY-ERNEST DEBORD, *Internationale Lettriste* No. 3 (August 1952)

113 | THE TRIBE

Surrealism. I myself didn't know much. I had read things here and there, some Breton, but not the political writings; I had read Prévert, Queneau—but they were not exactly Surrealists. And, like everybody from a Stalinist background, I knew Éluard and Aragon—even some of their early works. But for me the Surrealists were more of a myth: old-timers who had tried to do things but failed.

That was your view at that time?

Yes, but you have to bear in mind that I was perfectly capable of condemning someone without having read a single line of their work. I could hold forth for two hours about some film, some individual ... but I had a completely honorable reason for doing so: getting my drinks paid for. In bars you learn to follow several conversations at once, and I would listen to what people were saying.... The only film I remember seeing during that period is *Rashomon.* It was Michèle Bernstein who took me to see it on the Boul' Mich'. I think that was the only time I went to the movies in one or two years—we didn't go and see things, we didn't need to.

You mean you never went to the movies?

No, we didn't. Maybe Guy went now and again, alone, to see some particular thing, but the rest of the group hardly ever went, or if we went we didn't go to watch the film.

But didn't the Letterists—Isou, Wolman, Debord—play quite a significant role in film in the years 1950 to 1952?

Debord's film was perfect. I saw Gil's *L'Anticoncept* only much later, at Beaubourg, but I had read the script in *Ion.* I found it very beautiful. For me in those days film, just like the other forms of art, was completely outmoded—our task was to find something else. In the Letterist perspective, however, I was ready to make a film, too. I had even begun scribbling down a few sentences, but, of course, I lost them some night getting drunk somewhere or other. So I never became a filmmaker. Had I done so, I would have liked to make a film like Dufrêne's, without images, without anything.

It was nonetheless a leaflet against Chaplin that signaled the break between the left wing of Letterism and Isou.

Yes, yes, but it wasn't so much as a film actor or director that we denounced Chaplin. It was because he had accepted a medal from the police chief—that was what was completely unacceptable. We had to demolish Charlie Chaplin, but it was a directly political issue.

Same thing in the case of Breton: he was attacked on political grounds—because he had not behaved well in the broadest perspective.

Meaning?

We didn't know exactly, we didn't have all the details, but he had been on the radio in the United States during the war, and naturally everyone said that it was a CIA radio station, or things to that effect. At all events, Surrealism as we perceived it at that time was gaga, nothing but internal squabbling, a pale shadow of its former self.

And in a sense you represented the changing of the guard?

Absolutely. And I really do believe that there was a vacuum at that moment, politically speaking. Later

FINIS LES PIEDS PLATS

Cinéaste sous-Mack Sennett, acteur sous-Max Linder, Stavisky des larmes des filles mères abandonnées et des petits orphelins d'Auteuil, vous êtes Chaplin, l'escroc aux sentiments, le maître-chanteur de la souffrance.

Il fallait au Cinématographe ses Delly. Vous lui avez donné vos oeuvres et vos bonnes oeuvres.

Parce que vous disiez être le faible et l'opprimé, s'attaquer à vous c'était ·atta quer le faible et l'opprimé, mais derrière votre baguette de jonc, certains sentaient déjà la matraque du flic.

Vous êtes"celui-qui-tend-l'autre-joue-et-l'autre-fesse" mais nous qui sommes jeunes et beaux, répondons Révolution lorsqu'on nous dit souffrance.

Max du Veuzit aux pieds plats, nous ne croyons pas aux "persécutions absurdes " dont vous seriez victime. En français Service d'Immigration se dit Agence de Publicité. Une conférence de Presse comme celle que vous avez tenue à Cherbourg pourrait lancer n'importe quel navet. Ne craignez donc rien pour le succès de Limelight.

Allez vous coucher, fasciste larvé, gagnez beaucoup d'argent, soyez mondain (très réussi votre plat ventre devant la petite Elisabeth), mourez vite, nous vous ferons des obsèques de première classe.

Que votre dernier film soit vraiment le dernier.

Les feux de la rampe ont fait fondre le fard du soi-disant mime génial et l'on ne voit plus qu'un vieillard sinistre et intéressé.

Go home Mister Chaplin.

l'Internationale Lettriste :

SERGE BERNA   JEAN-L. BRAU

GUY-ERNEST DEBORD   GIL J WOLMAN

ANTI-CHAPLIN LEAFLET

on, the Surrealists unquestionably played an important role with the "Manifesto of the 121" during the war in Algeria. But if memory serves, Breton had compromised himself by dabbling in the Citizens of the World movement. We had this idea of Breton as in a way fallen; and if we hated him so much, perhaps it was not only that he was a father figure, but also that he was a father fallen from grace. There must have been something of that in it.

Once we went on a long expedition to interrupt the vernissage of a Surrealist exhibition at the Étoile Scellée gallery. I was with Jean-Louis Brau—Bull Dog Brau. "Bull Dog" was a sobriquet such as boxers had. There was a time when we all used two first names. I already had two, so nothing changed there, but Berlé was called "Pierre-Joël," Debord "Guy-Ernest," Wolman "Gil J," and Brau "Bull Dog"— because he was always talking about boxing. That was one of his great methods of striking up conversations in bars and getting treated. He would break in whenever guys were talking about boxing and could carry on for hours about it. I don't remember how it came about that he knew so much about boxing. Anyway, we were on this long mission, and we must have stopped at twenty-five bistros en route, and we were drinking Legros cocktails, which were absolutely lethal.

What is a Legros cocktail?

It's quite simple: you take a pastis, but instead of adding water you add rum. Occasionally, we would also add Cynar—a ghastly concoction, some kind of Italian aperitif flavored with artichokes—to spice the thing up a little. That day we were drinking one each time we stopped at a bar, and, of course, we ended up in the police station long before we got to the Étoile Scellée gallery. Anyway, we denied

NO MORE FLAT FEET
Sub–Mack Sennett filmmaker, sub–Max Linder actor, Stavisky of weeping unwed mothers and little orphans of Auteuil, hail Chaplin, swindler of emotions, master-singer of suffering.
The cinematograph needed its Dellys. You have given it your works—and your good works.
Since you claimed to stand for the weak and the oppressed, attacking you seemed like attacking the weak and the oppressed; but some have discerned the cop's nightstick behind the rattan cane.
You are "he who turns the other cheek and the other ass cheek," but we are young and good-looking, and when we hear suffering we reply Revolution.
You are a Max du Veuzit with flat feet, and we do not believe in the "absurd persecutions" you say you are the victim of. The French for immigration service is advertising agency. The kind of press conference you gave at Cherbourg would turn a complete dud into a sensation, so you needn't worry about the success of *Limelight*.
Go to bed, you budding fascist. Make lots of money. Mingle with high society (bravo for the groveling before little Elizabeth). Die soon, we can guarantee you a first-class funeral.
May your latest film be your last.
The footlights have melted the make-up of the supposedly brilliant mime. All we can see now is a lugubrious and mercenary old man.
Go home Mister Chaplin.
THE LETTERIST INTERNATIONAL:
SERGE BERNA
JEAN-L. BRAU
GUY-ERNEST DEBORD
GIL J WOLMAN

THE NIGHT OF CINEMA

The history of the cinema is full of
corpses with a high market value.
While the crowds and the intelligentsia
are yet again discovering old man
Chaplin or slavering with admiration
for the latest of Luis Buñuel's
Surrealist remakes, the ravages of the
Letterists, who are young and good-
looking, proceed apace:
Screens are mirrors that petrify the
adventurous by returning their own
images to them and halting them in
their tracks. If one cannot pass through
the screen of photography to something deeper, then the cinema holds no
interest for me.
Jean-Isidore Isou
April 1951: Treatise on Slobber
and Eternity

The time of the poets is over
Today I sleep
Gil J Wolman
February 1952: The Anticoncept
(banned by the censor)

"With my eyes closed I buy everything
at Au Printemps"
Guy-Ernest Debord
June 1952: Howls in Favor of Sade

In preparation:
The Boat of Ordinary Life
by Jean-Louis Brau
On the Mild Laughter Surrounding
Death
by Serge Berna

We make revolution in our spare time

Surrealists any right to continue presenting themselves as such in the neighborhood galleries. We
were, in any case, duty bound to denounce the
Surrealists. Which reminds me that we used to run
into an old gentleman who was Tristan Tzara. When
we met him, we would insult him.

Where did you use to see him?

At Le Bouquet, mainly. He used to play chess there.
There were three steps up to go in, a few tables and
chairs and chess players who stayed there all day
long. Le Bouquet was on the corner of Rue des
Ciseaux and Rue du Four—about thirty meters
from Moineau's.

Do you recall the type of insults you used?

Pretty crude, I suspect. We insulted him more as a
Dadaist than as a Stalinist—that was always the way:
Dadaists, Surrealists, they were our prime enemies.
Tzara was a Stalinist as well, of course—he had
been in the Communist Party for ages.

You hadn't read Tzara, I presume?

I don't know. Maybe one or two things from the
anthology....

Which did not prevent you from insulting him.

Certainly not. I insulted Péret, I hadn't read Péret,
and now I think Péret was one of the very, very
great. I also used to insult a much less well-known
guy by the name of Iliazd, usually at the Bonaparte,
a bar where he would go, because we were not ready
to acknowledge that he had produced poetry in the
twenties that was remarkably akin to Letterism.

La Nuit du Cinéma

L'histoire du cinéma est pleine de morts d'une grande valeur marchande. Alors que la foule et l'intelligence découvrent une fois de plus le vieillard Chaplin et bavent d'admiration au dernier remake surréaliste de Luis Bunuel, les lettristes qui sont jeunes et beaux poursuivent leurs ravages :

Les écrans sont des miroirs qui pétrifient les aventuriers, en leur renvoyant leurs propres images et en les arrêtant.
Si ont ne peut pas traverser l'écran des photos pour aller vers quelque chose de plus profond, le cinéma ne m'intéresse pas

Jean-Isidore **ISOU**

Avril 1951 :
TRAITÉ DE BAVE ET D'ÉTERNITÉ

C'est fini le temps des poètes
Aujourd'hui je dors

Gil **J WOLMAN**

Février 1952 :
L'ANTICONCEPT
(interdit par la censure)

« Les yeux fermés j'achète tout au printemps. »

Guy-Ernest **DEBORD**

Juin 1952 :
HURLEMENTS EN FAVEUR DE SADE

En cours de réalisation :
LA BARQUE DE LA VIE COURANTE
de Jean-Louis **BRAU**

DU LÉGER RIRE QU'IL Y A AUTOUR DE LA MORT
de Serge **BERNA**

NOUS FAISONS LA RÉVOLUTION
A NOS MOMENTS PERDUS

Would it be fair to say, then, that bad faith was part and parcel of the tribe's attitude?

Oh, it would be quite fair. In all good faith, I acknowledge that bad faith was part and parcel....

What effect did it have on you years later, when you had taken a very different path—first as a Communist and then as a Trotskyist militant—when you heard Debord's name mentioned in public?

I tried to keep up somewhat, but I don't think I can have read *The Society of the Spectacle* until twenty years after it was published. One day, though, I finally decided to read it. As for Debord's *Mémoires*, I can't recall when the book came out, but I must have read it very much earlier than *The Society of the Spectacle*.

Mémoires *was published in '58.*

Well, I didn't read it in '58, but someone lent it me later and I read it quickly. It dealt with our period— there was the photo of Éliane on her barstool, and one of me with Éliane and Pépère just back from Cayenne....

Did the book awaken your feelings from that time?

Yes, a touch of nostalgia, a touch of melancholy. And it reflected many things, including an aspect—well, let me put it this way: had you walked into Moineau's in those days, there were moments when you would have thought, "Why, these people, these young people are perfectly charming." Because we would sing a lot of songs. Midou would play the guitar from time to time, very sweetly. And we *were* sweet—even if it was solely due to our smoking

"JCR = cretins"
"Their knowledge of life owed nothing to their episodic presence in the precincts of the university nor yet to the few diplomas they had acquired by the most varied and least acknowledgeable means."

"What's your scene, man?"
"Reification."
"Yeah? I guess that means pretty hard work with big books and piles of paper on a big table?"
"Nope. I drift. Mostly I just drift."

FROM THE SITUATIONIST COMIC STRIP, *LE RETOUR DE LA COLONNE DURUTTI* (1966).
THE COWBOYS' EXCHANGE IS A *DÉTOURNEMENT* OF MICHÈLE BERNSTEIN'S NOVEL, *TOUS LES CHEVAUX DU ROI*
(PARIS: ÈDITIONS BUCHET/CHASTEL, 1960).

hash and drinking. We favored quite a few medieval songs, "Le Roi Renaud," things like that. People didn't know those then. And lots of Mac Orlan. Our favorite singer, even then, was Germaine Montero—I think I was the one who introduced "La Complainte de Margaret" and various similar things. Guy had this slightly retro side, and he liked these songs. "Bernard, Bernard, this green youth"— that side of Debord, his "reactionary" side, if you like, the refusal of the modern world. Old Paris, old houses, old you-name-it—and old songs. Gil, too, liked such things.

To get back to Guy's history, I didn't keep up at all. I was very surprised in May 1968—I couldn't imagine Guy surrounded by three thousand people; that wasn't his style at all. After that I did keep up more, but in 1968 Situationism was, after all, the enemy—though not for me so much, because I wasn't in the university, I wasn't a student, I was much too old. In 1968 we considered Situationism to be anti-Marxist. Which was wrong, of course, because in the meantime Guy had obviously read and studied Marx, and was trying to transcend Marx; the Marxist starting point in Debord is plain to see. But Situationism was spontaneist, a danger for the Trotskyists, who were organized, Leninists—well, in short, Situationism was anti-Leninist, and therefore Guy was our enemy. Personally, I was never bothered by this. I had nothing to do with what was said or not said by young Trotskyist comrades who were eighteen or twenty years old in '68 and who thought Situationism was nothing more than a group of people who had taken over some university building or other. They saw Situationists as political adversaries of the moment, but they knew absolutely nothing of their antecedents.

Did they know of your own past?

When I joined, no. They had no idea that I had once known Debord. Except for a few friends—but the subject rarely came up. Remember, too, that there was not much of a connection between the Debord I had known when we were hanging about together and what had now become a vast horde of Situs, pro-Situs, post-Situs—a horde that even Debord, as I understood it, did not care much for.

Were the Situationists very strongly opposed to your Trotskyist group, the Jeunesse Communiste Révolutionnaire (JCR)?

Yes, we were the enemy. In some university departments, the two groups were literally at daggers drawn. Later, gradually, I let it be known how I had once known Guy in quite different circumstances; but since during that whole period I gave everyone, including the Trotskyists, the impression that I was an individualist and a crank, they were not especially surprised. But we were now in 1968, more than fifteen years later. When I knew Debord most of the kids of May '68 were just toddlers. Between me and the youngsters in the high-school action committees there was a whole world, a chasm a century or two wide. Little by little the gap narrowed, and today when I see those same people, who are now about fifty as compared with my sixty-three, we are almost the same age. At the time, though, I must have seemed to them like a prehistoric monster. Most of them had never read *The Society of the Spectacle*—and still haven't. In their eyes the Situationists were simply an opposing political group—I'm even convinced that Vaneigem was better known to them than Guy, no doubt because there were ideas in Vaneigem that had an appeal for some of them,

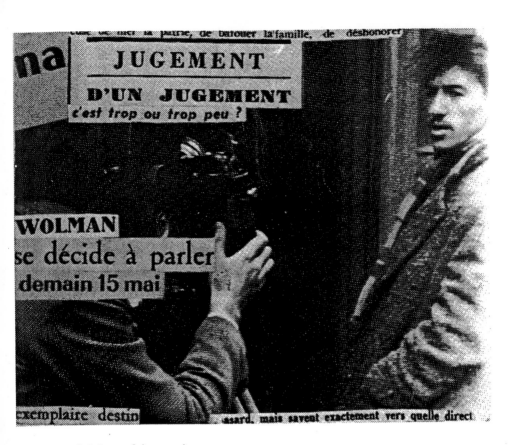

"Judgment of a judgment. Is it too much
—or too little? Wolman resolves to speak
tomorrow, 15 May."
Portrait of Gil J Wolman by
Guy-Ernest Debord

which was not true of Debord. Debord was simply
unfathomable, and they didn't understand a word.

Did you understand a word?

As I say, I hadn't read it at that time; I was too busy,
and we had our own stuff. But I caught up later and
revisited that past: I tried to reconstruct Guy's
development, and things began to gel—I could see
that he was still the same. Guy was a very tenacious
person, and he nurtured his memories. One might
be tempted to say that everything was already there
from the beginning. He was already very hard—

very strict in the way he conceived of coexistence with this person or that, but at the time I knew him, it seems to me, nothing was fixed, everything was still in movement. Moreover, there was a playful aspect to the way we lived, to the way our relationships were handled; and there was no competitiveness, not even with Brau—the group was pretty solid. Between Gil and Guy there was a division of spheres of action. I gather that, later on, hatreds emerged based on real differences, not on people simply falling out. There were certainly jokers who became part of Guy's group merely because they were friends of so and so, people who had no business there and who lasted only six months or a year before Guy found them really too idiotic and kicked them out. But in my time, the time of my friendship with Guy, everything was perfectly straightforward.

So when you came to read The Society of the Spectacle, *well after it appeared, you found passages echoing dicussions that you had had....*

Yes, yes—at the very least the same spirit, the same quest. I always took it as a given that Guy was pretentious, very pretentious—and rightly so. He played the game of transcending Marx, just as many people have tried to do, and in my opinion he did so more intelligently than others. In any case, he made a real contribution. I must have debated the transcendence of Marx I don't know how many times. The famous theories of play, of communication, etc.—all those mishmashes quickly faded away. As for Situationism, as for Guy's thinking, it is still with us. To my mind it doesn't in any way resolve the problem of revolution, but it remains a fairly consistent whole, and it certainly surpasses Marx on several counts.

Do you consider Guy Debord a moralist?

Yes. The last sentence of *In Girum* is: "Wisdom will never come." That's what makes Debord a good moralist, in my opinion.

The reference is to Ecclesiastes, isn't it?

I haven't read Ecclesiastes—my education didn't stretch to that! But Guy is a moralist in the sense that he gives very bad ideas to young boys and girls, which is a very good thing. And on that he never wavered. Very bad advice.

There are other phrases, too—like this, also from In Girum—*that must have touched you in particular: "It was great good fortune to have been young in this city when, for the last time, it shone with so intense a fire."*

Yes, indeed. I recognized Guy's particular way of thinking. I rediscovered our gang or part of it: several characters appear from the period Guy and I shared. And I rediscovered Guy's nostalgia.... In the end Guy was a sad person: he had a rather pessimistic vision of the future, even though that never prevented him from fighting. I don't know whether you could say he had a double personality, but I'm not at all sure that he really believed in the possibility of turning the world upside down; he believed absolutely in the necessity of trying to do so, on that he was categorical, but he was quite a pessimist.

Or this, from Panegyric: *"Between Rue du Four and Rue de Buci, where our youth went so completely astray, as we emptied a few glasses we could be quite sure we would never do anything better."*

That's it—we never have done any better. We have each done other things. But I do believe that I have never achieved anything better than the rebellion of that time.

"... for the very good reason that they had no craft, engaged in no study, and practiced no art"—that was the tribe, surely?

True. There were others in Moineau's who earned a wage—mainly for drinking purposes—people who had an occupation, more or less, but who didn't have the same ideas in their heads as we did, ideas about destroying this world. They simply thought that some day or other they had taken a tiny step which had brought them into this no man's land. Everyone in that place was marginal.

Wouldn't you say that everyone there was marginal and that very many of them stayed that way?

A good many of them, yes. "Never work!" was our absolutely universal watchword—one of the first to reappear at Nanterre in 1968. I remember one friend, René Leibé, who signed the leaflet "Hands Off the Letterists!" after Berlé's arrest in the Catacombs business. Leibé's fingernails must have been ten centimeters long, so determined was he to prove that he would never work. As for Guy, he succeeded, I gather, in working very little and living the life of the perpetual drinker and boozy thinker to perfection. For my part, I took a different route politically: I did work, unlike Guy, who says he never worked, but at bottom I think that we never changed. I still hold to the same positions, even if in my case they translate into quite different tactical political choices. The main thing is to persevere, to hold on to the end, the bitter end. For a century we

FRED AND JEAN-MICHEL
PHOTO: ED VAN DER ELSKEN/
THE NETHERLANDS PHOTO ARCHIVES

have been fooled by a parade of bureaucrats. Today we have a government that is more and more collaborationist and less and less class-based. No revolutionary tendency has succeeded in imposing itself. We have to put everything back on the table, take a fresh look at everything, and commit a kind of hara-kiri of the mind: everyone should rethink their ideas, their political agenda, from the ground up. This is not to say that everything that has been done has been useless. There is a solution, and we must find it together. I still embrace our ideas of old, still believe that we must absolutely destroy this world—not just because Marx said so, and not just because the working class is the only class that is revolutionary to the end, but because neither I nor, I think, Guy can live in this society. I have always remained marginal; I have always been a drunk....

Were there other formulations, like "Never work!" that came up over and over, that became leitmotifs or slogans that you all subscribed to?

There were a few phrases like that, and they are in the publications of the Letterist International. I remember my own: "The problem is not that they kill us, but that they make us live this way." And the only one that was always coming up, and that Gil quotes somewhere or other: "In any case, we won't come out alive." Those were two, and there were others, but often of the kind, "Chinese girls are Gaëtan's"—which was the leitmotif of Gaëtan M. Langlais, who quickly disappeared.

Were you looking for a family when you landed at Moineau's?

No, not a family; myself, I have always used the word "tribe." At that time the family was something

we scorned; of course, now, I see it a little different-
ly. But we had a kind of nostalgia for the past, for a
certain purity, a nostalgia that never remotely
approached any kind of mystical quest: the notion,
simply, that we were a little band of humans in the
middle of nowhere—there was something a bit
medieval about it.

Boccaccio-like?

A little, yes—a time before everything got really rotten. Generally, that was not the atmosphere around
the tribe, which was more like "let's go further, go
beyond, destroy, transcend." But occasionally there
would be this kind of contemplative moment ...
times when we rested briefly before mounting a
fresh assault on a couple more bottles and on the
world at large. And then, for a few moments each
day, we contrived to live almost like ordinary people. What I personally feel was the defining characteristic of the tribe, the thing that marked us off
completely from the regulars of all the other bars,
was this: at Moineau's, if someone had said—mind
you, you could say "I paint"—but if someone had
said, "I want to be a famous painter," if someone
had said, "I want to become a famous novelist," if
someone had said, "I want in whatever way to be a
success," then that someone would have been
tossed instantly out of the back room right through
the front room onto the street. There was an
absolute refusal of what you call—it wasn't even a
case of no Rastignacs, of no "I want a normal career"
as a painter, a writer, a what-have-you—it was a case
of all-out war. We rejected a world that was distaste-
ful to us, and we would do nothing at all within it. At
the same time, we wanted be the most intelligent
of all. We had simply no respect for anyone who
wanted to become established. The exception was

BARATIN AND JEAN-MICHEL. IN THE
MIRROR: OLD MADAME MOINEAU.
PHOTO: ED VAN DER ELSKEN/
THE NETHERLANDS PHOTO ARCHIVES

Renaud, a highly useful character because he had a little money. How Renaud came to be at Moineau's I can't imagine, because his ambition was to become a psychiatrist. His greatest passion, however, was to spend the weekend in Belgium, whence he hailed, observing mallards. He had written a thesis on *The Social and Sexual Habits of Mallards and Certain Other Anatidae.* I'll always remember that—ducks are the only animal family whose Latin name I know. I think his own sexual habits—well, I know you shouldn't call any sexual habits bizarre, but Renaud liked...

Ducks?

Not ducks, actually—I don't know exactly what he did on those weekends. But during the week, when he was in Paris, what he liked was lesbians. Why not, after all? He was a really lovely guy. He had us all take Rorschach tests—you know, the blotches. Just for fun—we didn't give a damn, of course, and neither did he. As for me, he told me that I would never be serious.

He wasn't entirely wrong there.

Not, not entirely. Another time he told me something very interesting: "If you don't want to be treated, no one can treat you." Why, that's perfect, I told him. That way, I can stay as I am.

GÉRARD BERRÉBY AND JEAN-MICHEL MENSION AT MARIE-JO'S BISTRO,
À L'AMI PIERRE, RUE DE LA MAIN D'OR, PARIS
PHOTO: GASTON

These interviews were conducted
between 15 January and 4 March 1997 in
the following cafés: Le Mabillon, Le Mazet,
La Palette, Le Saint-Séverin, La Chope,
and Au Petit Chez Soi.

The author and publisher wish to thank
the following for their precious help:
Grégoire Bouillier, Renaud Burel,
Ginette Dufrêne, François Escaig, Louis
Garans, Raymond Hains, Jacques Kébadian,
Sonia Kronlund, François Letaillieur,
Giulio Minghini, Jacques Moreau aka the
Marshal, Oro Pekelman, Maurice Rajsfus,
Jacques de la Villeglé, and
Charlotte Wolman.